Interdisciplinary Approaches
to Canadian Society

Interdisciplinary Approaches to Canadian Society

A Guide to the Literature

Edited by

A L A N   F . J .   A R T I B I S E

Published for the Association for
Canadian Studies
by McGill-Queen's University Press
Montreal & Kingston • London • Buffalo

ISBN 0-7735-0763-9 (cloth)
ISBN 0-7735-0788-4 (paper)

Legal deposit third quarter 1990
Bibliothèque nationale du Québec

(∞)

Printed in Canada on acid-free paper

This publication was made possible thanks to a grant
from the Department of the Secretary of State of
Canada and with the assistance of the International
Council of Canadian Studies.

Canadian Cataloguing in Publication Data
Main entry under title:
Interdisciplinary approaches to Canadian society

Includes bibliographical references.
ISBN 0-7735-0763-9 (bound).–
ISBN 0-7735-0788-4 (pbk.).

1. Canada. 2. Canada – Social conditions.
I. Artibise, Alan F.J., 1946-

FC95.I54 1990   971   C90-090305-8
F1021.2.I68 1990

The Association for Canadian Studies wishes to dedicate this book to the memory of the women who died at the Université de Montréal on 6 December 1989.

Contents

*Interdisciplinary Approaches
to Canadian Society*

CHAPTER ONE

Introduction: Canadian Society, Interdisciplinary Approaches

WALLACE CLEMENT

Canadian society is a complex social formation: it is considered part of the "new" world from a European perspective, yet indigenous people have been here since before recorded history. While Canada is a part of North America, it differs significantly from the United States, even though the two countries have much in common in terms of their economy, politics, and popular culture. Outstanding in Canada is the political and cultural presence of Quebec, with a majority Francophone population. The fact that Canada is an immigrant society is also noteworthy; this has meant an ethnically mixed society wherein many members have resisted the dominant trend toward Anglo-conformity (at least partly aided in that direction by the struggles of Canada's Francophone populations). The federal structure of government accords considerable power to the provinces (again especially protected by Quebec), including control over education, social services, and labour relations and resources, and has facilitated strong regional differences within Canada. Such differences are manifest, for example, in different traditions within the labour movement, which itself has been built upon diverse labour forces in resource extraction, concentrated industrial centres, and, more recently, an organized public sector.

Likely the most striking feature of Canadian society is the presence of "two nations" (one English-speaking, the other French-speaking); overlying this is the fact of Canada's being an immigrant society, with about a third of its population tracing its ethnicity to other than British or French origins. This diversity makes Canada more interesting than more homogeneous countries, but it is also a source of political and social tension. As each of the sections in this collection quite frankly expresses, the French of Quebec are handled, to varying degrees, distinctly from the rest of the country. This distinctive treatment reflects a real difference in both scholarly reality and socio-cultural experiences within Canada.

The Canadian studies community, both at home and abroad, is well served by the following collection covering four key subjects in the field. Most impressive, I believe, is the comprehensive coverage in one volume of both French- and English-language literatures, perspectives, and issues. With the exception of two pieces (on native studies), the articles are jointly authored by Anglophone and Francophone scholars in an unprecedented collaborative effort. It should be stressed, however, that the collaboration does not reduce the two linguistic scholarly communities to the same core; instead, the reader is offered an original and innovative view of the differences. Any reader who works through the pieces included here will surely conclude that there is a quality of scholarship in Canada worth sharing.

Not only has the strength of Canadian studies enhanced the substantive focus upon Canadian society; equally important has been its interdisciplinary contribution – it has been a way of breaking through restrictive disciplinary boundaries. An excellent example is the revival of interest in Harold Adams Innis, the historical economist whose work was more often cited outside than inside Canada until the late 1970s. Innis's work was largely ignored in Canada by professional historians, and especially by economists. The renewed interest in Innis's work coincides with the revival of political economy in Canada which transcends the traditional disciplinary bounds and recalls the more holistic writings of like-minded scholars. But their work was (and is) also valuable because of its substantive contribution. Canada, it turns out, is an interesting country to study and a challenge to understand, as those whose interests span geography, literature, history, and the social sciences generally agree. What Canadian studies has taught us is that insights can make valuable contributions across disciplines. Interdisciplinary work enriches, enlarges, and enlivens our understanding of Canada.

Interdisciplinarity does not mean "reducing to the lowest common denominator," or an elimination of perspectives and politics. As the chapter on labour clearly indicates, political perspectives inform (we might even say structure) the way interdisciplinary projects are undertaken. Interdisciplinarity has served to transcend and integrate, but, equally important, it has helped to humanize the social sciences and make the arts more analytical.

Canadian studies remains, for the most part, disciplinary research on Canada, with interdisciplinarity less common than many would wish. There are notable exceptions, such as the University of Waterloo's undergraduate program and, to some extent, Carleton University's graduate program. Few scholars, however, are employed as Canadian studies appointments. For the most part, we have sustained ourselves within disciplines from which we then choose to interact with other Canadianists. A notable institutional exception has been *The Journal of Canadian Studies*, located at Trent University (an institution that has done much to promote Canadian studies). JCS has been providing Canadian scholars and readers with a valuable forum for over twenty years. More recently established has been the Association for Canadian Studies, the organization sponsoring this publication, which emerged from the Canadian studies "movement" in the mid-1970s both to develop Canadian content within the colleges and universities and to challenge the traditional boundaries of disciplines. The history of the ACS, and its attractiveness, has been that its content is interdisciplinary as much as it is Canadian.

The depth of interdisciplinary content under the banner of Canadian studies, as revealed in this volume, is outstanding. There is no paper on politics, yet the papers reek of such matters; there is no paper on culture, yet it is peppered throughout the contributions; no section is devoted to social structure, regionalism, French-English relations, Canadian history, but all of these subjects are integral to the four topics – a most impressive accomplishment!

If Canadian studies has provided one major impetus toward interdisciplinarity, women's studies has provided the other. Each has challenged traditional disciplines and caused a re-evaluation of their assumptions and practices, both in scholarly terms and in terms of the politics of who practises the disciplines (that is, the presence of women and Canadians in major research and teaching positions). Both Canadian studies and women's studies have been political movements as well as paradigmatic challenges. They have called for new ways to examine and understand.

The challenge to Canadian studies (and women's studies) is to raise the level of analysis beyond the empirical; that is, to examine and critically evaluate the assumptions or paradigms dominant in the disciplines *and* in the society. Broadly, it is to reflect on *and* to educate people on how they can transform Canadian society. This means more than treating Canada or women as subjects. It means realizing the difference each makes for analysis and for how we understand our subjects.

Each of the papers in this collection takes a somewhat different approach to its subject, yet there is an astounding continuity and integrity to the pieces. The chapter on labour studies by Jacques Ferland, Gregory Kealey, and Bryan Palmer, for example, takes seriously studies of women and of the cultural dimensions of the working class. Its substantive weakness follows from its critique of social-democratic approaches to labour institutions, leaders, and events. Consequently, the chapter has little to say about federal-provincial jurisdictional issues and their implications for labour relations, or about the institutional structure of the labour movement as embodied in, for instance, the Canadian Labour Congress. Traditionally, the Canadian labour movement has been divided between its national and so-called international (meaning us-based) unions, with the us unions having a dominant place in the politics of labour. In the 1980s, however, there has been a definite movement toward Canadianization, dramatically signalled by the Canadian Automobile Workers' split from the United Automobile Workers in the United States. This movement has been spreading, and has had the consequence of transforming the political stance of the labour central, the Canadian Labour Congress, on key issues such as its opposition to free trade with the United States. Overall, the reader will be well rewarded by this chapter, which gives an excellent taste of what has been going on in research and debates within the field of labour studies. It is a lively analysis that takes the reader to the heart of this field in both French-Canadian and English-Canadian writings.

Donald Avery and Bruno Ramirez's chapter "Immigration and Ethnic Studies" is a masterpiece of multidisciplinary work. It combines in a short space the sense of both the literature and the subject in quite a brilliantly crafted piece. There are, of course, some subjects that receive little attention, such as the early Acadian experience and the Antigonish movement which followed, or the role of the Chinese labourers in the building of railways and in early fish-packing plants, but overall the chapter strongly conveys the relationship between immigration, ethnicity, and the building of a labour force. As I argued earlier, immigration and ethnicity are features of Canadian society which have made it distinctive (and interesting). They are also of major contemporary relevance. While the 1970s may have featured an ethnic revival in Canada, the 1980s have kept the issues alive through the politics of refugees, whether from southeast Asia, Eastern bloc countries, Latin America, or the Indian sub-continent. Canada has never been entirely consistent in its treatment of newcomers. There have always been the contradictions of welcoming and degradation, of promoting distinctiveness and demanding conformity. These tensions persist because Canada itself is not homogeneous and of "one mind," so its citizens' practices reflect, at various times, both racism and humanitarianism.

There are two contributions in the collection on the subject of native studies, the first by John A. Price and the second by Richard Dominique. They vary considerably in content and style. While Price's contribution is very informative, almost encyclopedic, it lacks some of the "zest" of the other articles. (Professor Price unfortunately died before he was able to undertake final revisions.) Dominique focuses on a critical assessment of the weaknesses in native studies within Quebec, and his paper is posed at a fairly general and abstract level, dealing with the logic of inquiry issues but offering little by way of the substantive or descriptive. This is in very stark contrast to Price's richly detailed survey. Neither deals significantly with the Métis people – who comprise a quarter of the native population in Canada – even though they have been subjected to some exciting analyses which combine patriarchy, class, and imperialism. The Métis are the creation of the fur trade, the vivid human expression of so many relationships, and are particularly important for locating issues ranging from the rights of native women to land claims. Canada's native people, as the contributions make clear, are not themselves homogeneous in their cultural practices and lifestyles. To some extent they have been forced to construct common political positions in seeking to resist the invasions of industrial society and to demand rights from the political process. Natives have been forced to create social movements to protect their special place as indigenous peoples in a land in which the dominant groups are all invaders. Over the past decade they have become more adept at using the courts and political processes to express their demands, but it appears that the most effective weapon at their disposal remains the protest, a technique they have mastered.

The outstanding paper on religion by Guy Laperrière and William Westfall is a model of interdisciplinarity. It is strong on religion and politics, regionalism, and the national question. It reveals the myriad of ways in which religion has had an impact on Canadian culture, ranging from education to architecture, and integrates the literature in both French and English. Although the piece could have developed some contemporary social issues, such as the Catholic bishops' important statement on the crisis in the Canadian economy, it does tackle a wide range of matters associated with religion both historically and in contemporary society. The authors make it clear that religion once was the core of interdisciplinarity in Canada, standing at the centre of politics, education, and culture. Today, while religion has declined as a practice and certainly has suffered a decrease in its position of power, it remains an important social force and a rich area of scholarship. Readers will be rewarded by the breadth of material covered in this chapter.

CONCLUSION

Few have been so ambitious as John Porter in the scope of his work in *The Vertical Mosaic* (Toronto: University of Toronto Press 1965), a classic work which pioneered the field of Canadian studies, positing that ethnicity had a central role in stratifying class and power structures – in other words, a "macrosociological" approach to Canadian society. Most of us have to be satisfied with more modest projects than a "total society" viewpoint. Such undertakings, however, are enriched by their location in a broader interdisciplinary context. Whether readers are students of Canadian society or non-Canadians with an interest in Canada, they will find value in the insights offered in the following essays, which are not only about Canada but treat Canadian subjects in an interdisciplinary manner. Those who have struggled to establish women's studies (both as an institution and through content in particular courses) will know the barriers of discipline that have confronted Canadian studies (within Canada).

In large part these have been surmounted in Canada, and a new agenda led by demand from abroad now needs to be satisfied. It is these twin audiences – students of Canadian studies here and those with an interest from abroad – that are addressed by giving them something of what we have learned about Canadian society. This collection is such a primer in the field, and a guide to further pursuits. Its users will welcome it as an effective introduction to an exciting country.

CHAPTER TWO

Labour Studies

JACQUES FERLAND, GREGORY S.
KEALEY, AND BRYAN D. PALMER

Labour studies programs, as such, exist in only a few Canadian colleges and universities. Instead, labour is studied within many disciplines as a specific sub-field – industrial relations, industrial sociology, labour law, labour economics, labour history, and so on. In the few institutions in which labour studies programs do exist, they tend to be a form of labour education, which in Canada is far more commonly controlled by the trade-union movement itself. This estrangement between the labour movement and higher education developed largely because of the role of academic experts in helping to solve "the labour problem." As "hired guns" for employers or government, academics historically have been viewed by labour leaders with hostility and suspicion.

For the purposes of this review, labour studies is defined broadly to encompass various disciplinary approaches, but, in general, this essay focuses on studies of the working class, not just of the labour movement, and on material which places the working class in historical perspective.

At the outset, three important peculiarities of Canadian working-class development should be noted. First, the Canadian trade-union movement has, for much of its history, been heavily influenced by United States labour. The Knights of Labor, the American Federation of Labor, the Congress of Industrial Organizations, and even the Industrial Workers of the World all organized on both sides of the forty-ninth parallel, paying little or no attention to the national border. While potentially a testimony to international working-class solidarity, too often the relationship degenerated into autocratic orders from US headquarters. Nevertheless, the phenomenon of "international unions," as they have euphemistically been known, is an important particularity of Canadian labour history. Second,

English-French tensions and regionalism have created major impediments to the emergence of a national labour movement. The simple fact that labour relations is a provincial power within Canadian federalism means that although there is a recognizable Canadian industrial-relations system, there are significant variations from jurisdiction to jurisdiction. While they are a veritable gold mine for labour lawyers, such differences are a terrible nightmare for the labour movement. Third, the Canadian labour movement, as a result, has been fractured into a number of competing central organizations. The Canadian Labour Congress (CLC) is by far the largest of these central labour bodies, but it has been unable, since its creation in 1956, to unite all organized Canadian workers.

In the essay that follows, English Canada and Quebec are discussed separately – a bifurcation that reflects the nature of how the field of study has developed historically.

ENGLISH CANADA

More than twenty years ago, it was possible for historian Stanley Mealing to write of the study of class in Canada and to conclude that those who had approached the Canadian experience through a class analysis were both few in number and unlikely to produce any substantial re-interpretation of the country's historical development. Today, while some would still hold to the view that the study of labour has produced few new synthetic or analytic breakthroughs, none can deny that the working class has clearly arrived as a subject of considerable interest, controversy, and spirited debate.[1] This recent literature, which is at the very centre of scholarly production within history, is also increasingly significant in the fields of political economy, sociology, and economics, not to mention being a virtual growth industry in the area of industrial relations.

It is within Mealing's own historical discipline that labour studies have arguably been most influential and controversial. Almost no text on Canadian history now ignores "the labour question," especially for the much-studied periods of the first impact of industrial capitalism, in the late nineteenth century, and the years of labour revolt associated with the working-class agitations of 1919. Yet, as a section devoted to working-class history in Paul W. Bennett and Cornelius J. Jaenen's edited collection *Emerging Identities: Selected Problems and Interpretations in Canadian History* (Scarborough, Ont.: Prentice-Hall 1986, 321–46) indicates, there is little agreement among historians, little in the way of consensus about how to conceptualize labour's past.

This is so because within historical studies the examination of the working class is one of the most politically charged areas of study. An exploration of the major themes and approaches in the field reveals the ways in which the politics of historical practice, the selection of specific kinds of experience, and the hierarchical ordering of discrete periods and aspects of study all converge in particular orientations, uses of evidence, and conclusions.

The general field of labour history emerged late in Canada, and did not grow out of any well-established series of studies of labour economics, trade-union histories, and government-labour relations. Unlike both the United States and England, then, where the Wisconsin School of labour economics and a line of Fabian inquiry had, respectively, conducted just such examinations of labour's development, an academic labour history in Canada had few guidelines around which to structure its concerns. When labour history began to rear its head as an area of respectable academic inquiry in this country, its original character was dominated not so much by an engagement with the strengths and weaknesses of past approaches, but rather by the political context of the period of its gestation: the late 1940s and the 1950s.

These were the years of the Cold War and of a virulent anti-communism, fought out on one level within the labour movement itself. The first serious review of Canadian trade-union development, economist Harold A. Logan's *Trade-unions in Canada* (Toronto: Macmillan 1948), was published as this confrontation was coming to a head, providing an unmistakably partisan statement on behalf of one of the warring factions within the labour movement, the social-democratic Co-operative Commonwealth Federation (CCF). By depicting the CCF's major rival, the Communist Party of Canada, as an "imposition of foreign thought" disloyal "to acknowledged leaders of the unions," given to "the secret tactics of Fosterism," Logan's book helped to mould the thoughts of social-democratic intellectuals, such as historian Kenneth McNaught, in specific ways, reinforcing a conception of Canadian labour history that looked inward to the country's peculiarities rather than outward to labour's connections to Britain or the United States, or in the direction of analytic frameworks emerging in other national contexts.

More important, perhaps, the field of working-class history in this country was, from its inception, one of the most partisan intellectual endeavours imaginable. With the Cold War driving communists of all sorts into retreat, working-class history was, by default, increasingly social-democratic terrain, especially in its development within universities. And it was the political needs of the moment that loomed large in the first products of professional labour historians: working-class history assumed an established agenda with the study of trade unions, of social reform, and of the development of a humanistic leadership of the progressive movement, with labour itself topping the list of acceptable areas of scrutiny. McNaught's *A Prophet in Politics* (Toronto: University of Toronto Press 1959), a biography of J.S. Woodsworth, the father of Canadian social democracy and an important figure in the Winnipeg General Strike, was the exemplary study in this genre.

In the years after 1965, much of the original social-democratic commitment waned, and the sporadic and marginal character of writing on labour history was finally supplanted by a wave of published work. This new professionalization of labour history, would be rooted, however, in unquestioning acceptance of the institutional/ social-democratic approach that found expression in a deepening routinization of labour history, with studies focused almost exclusively on episodic events in labour's progressive march or on the large-scale contours of unionism's growth and political trajectory. Moreover, social democracy's conception of useful histories translated into a continuing presentism, with most of the new studies that were born in graduate work in the 1960s focusing on the post–World War I years that had direct relationship to either the social-democratic tradition or its often reluctant ally, the modern labour movement. One need only read the major texts of this period – Irving Abella's *Nationalism, Communism and Canadian Labour* (Toronto: University of Toronto Press 1973) and Bercuson's *Confrontation at Winnipeg* (Montreal: McGill-Queen's University Press 1974), to name but two that happened to have their origins in doctoral theses supervised by McNaught – to grasp the nature of the field at this time. McNaught himself has captured nicely its essential concerns in a more recent call for attention to what represents for him the *fundamental* matters of labour's history:

The lines along which future research might seek further explanation of this non-revolutionary tale should include detailed examination of the relationship between, on the one hand, real standards of living, social security, and collective bargaining rights, and, on the other, the growth and policies both of the unions and the CCF-NDP. While this blindingly innovative recommendation may come as small surprise, its acceptance would nevertheless contribute to a realistic assessment of the roles of leadership, militancy on the economic front, parliamentarianism, and extra-parliamentarianism. Those young researchers who have been lovingly adapting E.P. Thompson to the mines, production lines, and even the countryside of Canada's past might well recall the emphasis Clare Pentland placed upon educated lead-

ership when he was discussing the struggles and gains of the 1930s and
1940s: "The outcome was that, again, the competence gap between employers (managers) and workers had narrowed very dangerously, inviting
conflict between self-confident workers and defensive, unimaginative employers. The union leadership created in this period – which for many years
employers said was too smart for them – remained in office almost to the
present day." That smart union leadership was not the product of any
autonomous working-class culture. It grew out of an increasing sophisti-
cation and education. And its goal was not to defend an Archie-Bunker–
charivari culture but, rather, to liberate those who had been entrapped by
the economic-cultural constraints imposed by political capitalist. ("E.P.
Thompson vs. Harold Logan," *Canadian Historical Review* 62 (1981): 168)

If, then, the overt politics of social democracy occasionally succumbed, with McNaught, like many "liberals in a hurry" before him,
abandoning the social-democratic ship to board a federalist liberal-
ism, the premises of a labour history first conceived in the context
of the 1940s slipped unobtrusively into a new epoch. Indeed, the
conclusion to McNaught's article, quoted above, articulated the
social-democratic/institutional approach to labour studies, with its
stress on trade-union development, a respectable politics of labour,
and an uncritical approach to workers' leaders, that prevailed
throughout the 1960s and early 1970s. But different approaches to
the Canadian working-class experience began to be espoused in the
post-1975 years, as McNaught's implicit antagonism toward the "lov-
ing adaptation" of British historian E.P. Thompson to Canadian class
experience and his rather bizarre reference to "an Archie-Bunker–
charivari culture" indicate. These new approaches would set the
stage for a reassessment of working-class history, a sharpening debate within historical circles, and closer connections between historians and those in other disciplines.

The 1970s gave rise to a radical historical practice different from
the earlier social-democratic project. Untainted by the anti-com-
munism/anti-Marxism of the 1940s, the labour history that began to be developed in the 1970s and 1980s was a reflection of an
entirely different set of contexts and concerns. The young practitioners of what would come to be referred to as the "new labour
history" were participants in or direct followers of the campus revolts
of the 1960s. Attracted to events in Paris (1968), Prague (1968), or
Washington (1970), they feared no "foreign imposition" on their
intellectual development, but looked willingly to influences from
abroad and often enrolled in graduate programs in the United States
or England. Drawn to the renaissance of Marxism in the 1960s and
early 1970s, they were first struck with the general importance of

theory, looking to a series of developments within Western Marxism after 1917 for insight into the nature of class structure and the character of the subordination of the working class in capitalist societies, especially in the direction of writers like Antonio Gramsci. Many took inspiration from British and American studies (by E.P. Thompson, E.J. Hobsbawm, Eugene D. Genovese, David Montgomery, Harry Braverman, and Herbert G. Gutman) that appeared in the 1960s and 1970s and heralded a break with earlier histories of subordinate groups. Finally, the emergence of women's history, growing directly out of the rebirth of the women's movement in the 1960s which generated a revival of feminism, provided a third and complementary influence, forcing consideration of the process through which labour was reproduced in the family and socialized into productive relationships, stamped with the form and content of patriarchy.

What was different in this approach to working-class history was not so much what was studied – for trade unions and labour politics could still, of course, be examined – although that too would change. Rather, the key difference was in how labour was conceived. The focus was unmistakably on class formation rather than on union development, and the concern was less with a particular history of explicit political use than with working-class life in all of its complexities. Generally, those who were fashioning this kind of labour history in the late 1970s and early 1980s were driven by their commitment to write the social history of the working class, a broad project that did not necessarily call for the neglect of economic life, political activity, or institutional developments. If labour's material conditions, ideological development, electoral struggles, and trade unions were of essential importance in this broad social history, so too were hitherto unexplored aspects of workers' experience: family life, leisure activities, community associations, and work processes and forms of managerial domination affecting both the evolution of unions and the lives of unorganized workers. Even when products of this period abstained from theoretical comment, as in Judith Fingard's self-proclaimed descriptive account of labour in the shipping centres of nineteenth-century Canada, *Jack in Port* (Toronto: University of Toronto Press 1982), such studies inevitably stepped outside of the boundaries established by earlier institutional-political explorations of respectable social-democratic labour achievements, invariably carrying a series of "Thompsonian" concerns into the discourse on Canadian workers.

The diversity of this recent writing nevertheless deserves comment. Some published works – including Joy Parr's *Labouring Children* (Montreal: McGill-Queen's University Press 1980), an examination of the labouring experiences of pauper immigrant children; Bryan Palmer's *A Culture in Conflict, Toronto Workers Respond to Industrial Capitalism* (Montreal: McGill-Queen's University Press 1979), a discussion of skilled labour in Hamilton in the late nineteenth and early twentieth centuries; Gregory Kealey's *Toronto Workers Respond to Industrial Capitalism, 1867–1892* (Toronto: University of Toronto Press 1980), a similar study of Toronto workers; and *Dreaming of What Might Be* (New York: Cambridge University Press 1982), an account of the Knights of Labor in Ontario by Kealey and Palmer – attempt detailed monographic explorations of slices of working-class experience. Palmer's *Working-Class Experience: The Rise and Reconstitution of Canadian Labour, 1800–1980* (Toronto: University of Toronto Press 1983) provides a synthetic overview, while two recent collections – Craig Heron and Robert Storey's *On the Job* (Montreal: McGill-Queen's University Press 1986) and Bryan Palmer's *The Character of Class Struggle* (Toronto: McClelland and Stewart 1986) – are compilations of article-length studies reflecting concerns with the work process and class conflict. A host of other articles and postgraduate theses attest to the treatment of subjects that a previous labour history never envisaged, and break out of the older preoccupation with a past directly linked to present political concerns. Subjects of impressive recent studies include ritualistic forms of community resistance; patterns of craft inheritance among shoemakers; the place of the family economy in Montreal in the 1870s and 1880s; the riotous behaviour of early canalers; the significance of the life cycle among Quebec cotton workers (1910–1950); the nature of life in coal communities; and the role of literacy, housing, tavern life, and the oral tradition among specific groups of workers. Needless to say, the eclectic concerns of much of this new work, as well as diverging methods, ensure that this output lacks the coherence and structured direction of older approaches. While some of these examinations have concentrated on the structural, largely impersonal, dimensions of class life (the size of working-class families, the numbers of workers associated with sectors of the labour market, wage rates and levels of unemployment), other works have focused on the cultural activities of workers and the conflicts they have waged at the workplace or in the community.

Among this growing historical production, therefore, differentiation rather than homogeneity is apparent within the broad project of creating a social history of the working class. And it would be wrong to conclude, as well, that all work in the post-1975 output has left behind the institutional-political premises of an earlier age. Monographs such as Laurel Sefton MacDowell's *Remember Kirkland Lake* (Toronto: University of Toronto Press 1983), a study of the monumental strike of gold miners in northern Ontario in 1941–42;

Sally Zerker's *The Rise and Fall of the Toronto Typographical Union* (Toronto: University of Toronto Press 1982); Eugene Forsey's encyclopedic *Trade unions in Canada* (Toronto: University of Toronto Press 1982); and Desmond Morton's unashamedly social-democratic-inspired and institutionally focused survey, *Working People* (Ottawa: Deneau & Greenberg 1980) keep this approach very much alive. Not a little of this recent output, moreover, is openly agnostic in its refusal to enlist itself in any camp, an abstentionism that often makes sense and that pervades much feminist-inspired work that tacitly distances itself from the more overt advocates of both contending approaches.

Yet there is no denying that recent writing on Canadian working-class history, especially in its more polemical forms, has enlivened the entire profession, forcing an empirically oriented discipline to be more analytical, and demanding of theoretically poised histories that they be more rigorous and conceptually clear. Moreover, the political character of historical writing, so easily obscured and mystified, has been literally forced into the arena of debate and argument, as the early Marxist histories of Palmer and Kealey met sustained and unrestrained assault by the social-democratic guard dogs and champions of empiricism. While *A Culture in Conflict, Toronto Workers Respond to Industrial Capitalism*, and *Dreaming of What Might Be* were accorded a schizophrenic welcome in historical circles – simultaneously awarded accolades (Honourable Mention in the Macdonald Prize, the Macdonald Prize, and the Corey Prize, respectively) and being subjected to some of the nastiest reviews in the history of Canadian historical reviewing[2] – the particular focus of these works on skilled workers and on a culture of resistance to capitalism began to be challenged, not only by anti-Marxists, but by young Marxist historians such as Ian McKay. McKay laid less stress on the solidarities of working-class experience and more on the fragmentation and sectionalism associated with regional differentiation, labour-market segmentation, and the self-identifications of an aristocracy of workers within the craft community. These are themes that McKay has developed in articles on waterfront labour and on bakers in Victorian Halifax and, in subdued ways, in his recent study *The Craft Transformed: An Essay on the Carpenters of Halifax 1885–1985* (Halifax: Holdfast 1985).

Such interpretive differences, which are with each completed book and article receding in importance, are also at the centre of the intersection between labour history and political economy. The preoccupation of political economy, of course, has been Canadian dependency. Recent works by Leo Panitch and Daniel Drache, published in the journal *Studies in Political Economy*, highlight this disciplinary conjuncture, scrutinizing labour history to offer comments on how class formation and dependent development are related. Panitch focuses more on the ways in which the weakness of capital allowed a relatively strong working class to develop in central Canada, while Drache sees colonialism running rampant within the central Canadian working class, producing an enfeebled and xenophobic labour aristocracy that relied on state support to organize trade unions that were both exclusivist and racist. The point is not that political economists – like labour historians – can disagree or are capable of extreme interpretive formulations. Rather, what is apparent is the extent to which labour historians and political economists are now engaged in a collective endeavour, a project initiated by the now much-criticized but still impressive work of H.C. Pentland, published posthumously in 1981 as *Labour and Capital in Canada, 1650–1860* (Toronto: J. Lorimer 1981). While disagreements are many, never in the past have historians and political economists dealt with one another so directly through their conferences, journals, published texts, and left-wing journalism (à la *Canadian Dimension*). This process, evident in the *New Practical Guide to Canadian Political Economy* (Toronto: J. Lorimer 1985), edited by Daniel Drache and Wallace Clement, is also apparent in the increasing attention paid to the contemporary crisis in the labour movement by political economists and historians. Leo Panitch and Donald Swartz (*From Consent to Coercion: The Assault on Trade-union Freedoms*, Toronto: Garamond 1985) and Bryan Palmer (*Solidarity's Story: Reformism, the Fight Against the Right, and the Rise and Fall of British Columbia's Solidarity* (Vancouver: New Star 1986) address the current malaise of the working-class in ways that break decisively from the social-democratic reification of labour's leadership and the ahistorical glorification of the great working class victories of the 1940s.

Political economy embraces a broad range of disciplinary approaches, encompassing history, sociology, and economics. Among sociologists, Wallace Clement, formerly concerned with the corporate elite, has perhaps paid most attention to the Canadian working class, producing a study entitled *Hardrock Mining: Industrial Relations and Technological Changes at Inco* (Toronto: McClelland and Stewart 1981), as well as a series of more theoretical essays on proletarianization and property, most of which are drawn together in a collection, *Class, Power, and Property* (Toronto: Methuen 1983). One of the most useful union histories, Jerry Lembcke and William M. Tattam's *One Union in Wood: A Political History of the International Woodworkers of America* (Madeira Park, BC: Harbour 1984), is the product of two American sociologists, while James W. Rinehart's *The Tyranny of Work* (Toronto: Harcourt Brace Jovanovich Canada 1987) is a widely used sociological and historical survey of work and its discontents. A reflection of the burgeoning interest in the working class among sociologists is the bi-annual conference called "Workers and their Communities," which has now grown to a three-day affair encompassing some fifty distinct panels, round tables, and workshops involving hundreds of participants.

Nothing is more apparent, then, than the extent to which labour studies have become inter- or multi-disciplinary. While there are lines of demarcation separating historians, political scientists, and sociologists, they are becoming increasingly blurred. If historians of the working class are attracted to particular events and developments, devoting more energy to empirical research in original sources, even they are now drawn to large-scale generalization and synthetic statement, often resting on explicit theoretical formulations, as in Bryan Palmer's recent "Social Formation and Class Formation in Nineteenth-Century North America," in David Levine, editor, *Proletarianization and Family History* (Orlando: Academic 1984). Political economists, their academic ancestry rooted in Innis and staples theory, are, to be sure, often concerned with the particular weight of the resource sector in Canada and with external relations of trade and domination. However, their attention to class formation and its relationship to Canadian development can no longer be (if it ever was) reduced to the realm of exchange, and political economy is now centrally concerned, as are sociology and history, with productive relations, state policy, and the work process, as the work of Paul Craven, *An Impartial Umpire: Industrial Relations and the Canadian State, 1900–1911* (Toronto: University of Toronto Press 1980), makes clear.

To channel the approach to the working class along these lines to the exclusion of other relations and processes, however, would be to direct labour studies along particular gendered paths. Feminist work – historical, theoretical, sociological – has increasingly identified the interconnectedness of the productive and reproductive spheres, calling attention to the ways in which waged work and domestic labour are dichotomized only through an adoption of the very categories of the superficial and false separation that thrives in patriarchal conventional wisdom. Recent studies have focused on the forms of oppression and exploitation endured by working women structured into employer-created job ghettos, and on union reluctance to admit them to unambiguous membership. Pat Armstrong's *Labour Pains* (Toronto: Women's Educational Press 1984), Pat Armstrong and Hugh Armstrong's *The Double Ghetto: Canadian Women and Their Segregated Work* (Toronto: McClelland and Stewart

1984), Linda Briskin and Linda Yantz's edited collection *Union Sisters* (Toronto: Women's Press 1983), Jennifer Penney's compilation *Hard-Earned Wages* (Toronto: Women's Press 1983), and Paul Phillips and Erin Phillips' overview *Women and Work* (Toronto: Lorimer 1983) are among the many studies addressing these related themes. More challenging for labour historians in their implications are empirical studies of domestic work, such as Meg Luxton's *More Than a Labour of Love* (Toronto: Women's Press 1980) and the theoretically influential *The Politics of Reproduction* (Boston: Routledge & Kegan 1981) by Mary O'Brien, monographs which point to the need to consider the linkages between household and workplace, biology and class. Feminist analyses of the role of government legislation and dispensation of welfare in the stabilization of a class and of gendered social order also alert those interested in the working class to the critical role of state policy, a matter of fundamental importance in the vastly expanded industrial-relations field.

John A. Willes, in *Contemporary Canadian Labour Relations* (Toronto: McGraw-Hill Ryerson 1984), provides an introduction to industrial-relations themes and approaches, but the main point to stress in any appreciation of this area is the sheer volume of output and the eclectic concerns of the field, which range from how AIDS is affecting public-sector workers in the health-care sphere, through traditional labour histories and the mechanisms of grievance procedures, to youth unemployment and its future consequences. The *Index of Industrial Relations Literature*, published by the Industrial Relations Centre at Queen's University in 1984, cites 2,242 separate items that appeared in one year alone. Motivation and multinationals, labour law and labour mobility, profit sharing and productivity – all of these and an endless list of other subjects are the terrain of an industrial-relations field that has the funding and the sense of mission to imperialistically encroach on any and all areas of labour studies.

One area within this expansionist empire is concern with the important place of public-sector unionism, a phenomenon whose rise – dating from the early to mid-1960s – parallels that of industrial relations itself. A recent collection, edited by Mark Thompson and Gene Swimmer, is indicative of the way in which escalating militancy captivates attention, sweeping through disciplines and mobilizing comment upon a topic of considerable contemporary interest. The fifteen contributors to the text represent figures from faculties of business and commerce, industrial relations, law, economics, political science, and public administration. Overwhelmingly focused on the militant, strike-ridden, tension-laden history of public-sector unionism in Canada, the essays in this collection are an indication of how academics are drawn to the potential of a situation still very much unresolved in the eye of the public and in the concreteness of policy. As the title of this book, *Conflict or Compromise: The Future of Public Sector Industrial Relations* (Montreal: Institute for Research on Public Policy 1984), suggests, the study of labour is often an attempt to intervene directly in the choices and directions that will be taken in the years ahead.

What this strongly suggests is the eminently political and engaged character of labour studies in Canada. Indeed, it should come as no surprise that the single study that perhaps marks the take-off point for labour studies in modern Canada, Stuart Marshall Jamieson's *Times of Trouble: Labour Unrest and Industrial Conflict in Canada, 1900–1966* (Ottawa: Task Force on Labour Relations 1968), was a commissioned inquiry that grew out of an official state desire to comprehend the meaning of the working-class revolt of the mid-1960s. Labour studies in Canada, then, from Logan to Jamieson, from McNaught to Panitch, from Bercuson to Kealey, reflect the truth of British historian Richard Johnson's assessment that studies of the working class "only get written when the larger part of the population is held to matter enough to be an object of inquiry." And in the case of Canada it is apparent that how and why this larger population is held to be important is a basic determinant of just what kind of examinations of labour's past and present will be produced.

QUEBEC

Even though labour studies in Quebec have shown much more vitality since Jean Hamelin and Yves Roby inserted a chapter on capital and labour into their economic history *Histoire économique du Québec, 1851–1896* (Montreal: Fides 1971), anyone aware of the evolution of this field in recent years in English Canada would be struck by the tenacious concentration on the institutional and ideological manifestations of working-class experience in Quebec. Far from being superseded, or even complemented, by more basic social issues such as the specific modalities of social relationships of production, relations among workers in their communities and work environments, or the impact of inter-capitalist rivalries on labour, this focus on the "superstructural reverberations" of class struggles remains by far the dominant feature among the most widely published labour specialists. While new issues and theoretical frameworks are being introduced elsewhere, much of the literary production on labour in Quebec remains within the realm of trade-union studies, labour politics, and the *question nationale*.[3] Meanwhile, questions concerning the representativeness of these labour organizations and the relevance of this rhetoric for the whole labour force are not dealt with convincingly.

Such an inclination was already quite obvious when André E. Leblanc and James D. Thwaites published a retrospective bibliography in 1973 (*Le monde ouvrier au Québec*, Montreal: Les presses de l'Université du Québec). Most of the quantitative research on labour had stemmed from industrial relations, and, according to Gérard Dion, remained "more descriptive than analytical" and focused almost entirely on current events or topics of immediate interest.[4]

Among the most representative works of this earlier period are those of Louis-Marie Tremblay, Jacques Dofny, and Paul Bernard. Their published reports, commissioned by the federal government for the Task Force on Labour Relations, can be summarized as being only remotely interested with labour *per se*, interpreting labour relations through the structures of the two major federations of unionized workers (the Confédération des syndicats nationaux [CSN] and the Fédération des travailleurs du Québec [FTQ]) and their respective ideologies and rivalries.[5] These writers' tight equation of labour institutions with labour relations assumed that labour could be studied without any thorough study of the working class, which is another way of arguing that the initiative and impetus in these matters do not stem from the workers but from other social actors, such as the Catholic clergy and members of the Quebec intelligentsia, and from external influences.[6]

Nonetheless, some of our predecessors' works deserve a positive appraisal, especially those of Alfred Charpentier. His autobiography, *Cinquante ans d'action ouvrière: les mémoires d'Alfred Charpentier* (Quebec City: Les Presses de l'Université Laval 1971), is particularly valuable. Converted to Catholic unionism in 1918, Charpentier shares with us his experience as an organizer and as the president of the Confédération des travailleurs catholiques du Canada, including detailed accounts of the 1937 textile- and steel-workers' strikes and a "critical analysis" of the controversial 1949 asbestos strike. Admittedly, his memoirs overemphasize the influential individuals – politicians, capitalists, clergy, and union representatives – but his analyses of major strikes also refer to the rank and file and to what he believed to be the roots of their grievances. In short, this book, which should be read in conjunction with the relevant passages of Jamieson's *Times of Trouble*, remains an indispensable source for those who are not familiar with the labour movement in Quebec during the "torpid twenties," the "dirty thirties," and the most reactionary years of the Duplessis era.

It is precisely because of this tendency to ignore the workers in the superstructural approach to labour that the much scarcer publications focusing on labour conflicts are so valuable, since they have long been almost the only works offering the insights of those who were willing to risk a great deal in confronting wealth and authority. Whether written by economists, journalists, priests, lawyers, sociologists, or historians, these accounts of strikes or lock-outs always offer the opportunity to draw conclusions about the state of social relations in a crisis-ridden capitalist society. Needless to say, such statements are often equivocal, as a strike is not an easily grasped phenomenon. Rather, it is the exposed tip of the social relationships of production, a manifestation of an objective condition of conflict which remains open to conjectural statements as to its origin, outcome, and repercussions. Early publications on social antagonism between capital and labour in Quebec mostly centred on the period after World War II and, to a lesser extent, the 1930s. This is partly owing to the alleged pivotal role of the 1949 asbestos strike in the "emancipation" of Quebec society, a strike which did result in an unprecedented class polarization between nationalists, intellectuals, and workers, on the one hand, and an autocratic provincial government and an ethnocentric multinational corporation on the other.[7] Few of these authors, however, have given as much attention to the ordinary worker as Evelyn Dumas did so admirably in her *The Bitter Thirties in Quebec* (Montreal: Black Rose Books 1975),[8] a study of selected strikes in various industrial sectors between 1934 and 1944, inspired by "an ardent desire to learn from the very lips of the principal actors in various conflicts in Quebec history how they had lived these experiences."(p. 15). What is most significant about this little book is not its theoretical contribution – a rather timid attempt to interpret twelve strikes in the light of the works of A. Touraine and R. Bendix, among others – but that, for once, the historical initiative is given to the workers themselves rather than to institutions or key individuals.

Compared to these publications, and to others which appeared in periodicals such as *Relations industrielles* and *Parti Pris*, studies concerned with the emergence of class antagonism in the mid-nineteenth century, with the growing manifestation of a "labour problem" during the industrial revolution, and with the expansion of the labour movement at the turn of this century only began to appear in the early 1970s.[9] A new generation of historians, led by Jean Hamelin, attempted to fill this gap by publishing a "répertoire" of strikes in the province of Quebec during the nineteenth century, which was followed by what was, for the time, an ambitious synthesis entitled *Les travailleurs québécois 1851–1896* (Montreal: Les presses de l'Université du Québec 1975).[10] Although their primary aim was simply to reveal the facts "for their own sake," one cannot help making some sense of such facts. And by clearly distinguishing the history of the proletariat from the history of work and relegating the latter to future research, these facts were interpreted by relying on the economic conjuncture and on universal principles. In short, this was an untimely attempt to write a synthesis which could result only in broad, oversimplified statements about the social conditions of the working class and the perception of their movement essentially as a function of economic cycles. The central message, in this case, is that strikes should be perceived as temporary deviances from normal labour relations rather than as systemic confrontations between competing interests, removing again the historical initiative from the workers in given conjunctural periods.

Jacques Rouillard was unquestionably the most prolific, and probably the most prominent, author within this new generation of labour historians. Generally, his work clearly testifies to his everlasting fascination with labour institutions and their leaders, a dimension which cannot be taken as the starting point for labour history since, historically, these organizations have contained only a small fraction of the working class, and union practices have not always been genuinely concerned with the majority of non-unionized workers. This epistemological issue should not, however, diminish the intrinsic value of his contribution.

Rouillard's first book, *Les travailleurs du coton du Québec, 1900–1915* (Montreal: Les presses de l'Université du Québec 1974), is particularly noteworthy, as it represents the first published close-up of a collective of industrial workers – a collective truly representative of the Quebec work force – and because the author attempts to integrate these workers into their particular socio-economic milieu. At this point in his career, Rouillard was leading the way in a direction which has considerable potential for illuminating the drawbacks of the superstructural approach, wherein, frequently, all workers are perceived indiscriminately and almost all labour conflicts are assumed to be collective. Unfortunately, this short monograph does not shine sufficient light upon the intricacies of this particular collective of operatives, wherein a spinner may be either a child, a young female, a skilled mulespinner or his subordinate, or a piecer, and wherein the word "weaver" in French (*tisserand*) may designate not only a loom tender but a skilled mechanic who could be expected to act as a group leader by the foreman. Thus, with his emphasis on the militancy of mule-spinners (two per cent of the collective) and of the *tisserands* (i.e., loom-fixers – one per cent of the collective), Rouillard draws much attention away from the collective struggle of the less-skilled cotton workers for the sake of tiny groups of potential assistant-foremen aiming at wage parity with their New England counterparts.[11]

In his later publications, Rouillard turned his attention to national and international unions. His doctoral dissertation, published as *Les syndicats nationaux au Québec de 1900 à 1930* (Quebec City: Les presses de l'Université Laval 1979), makes a clear distinction between secular and confessional national unions, as the former never sought to reform the capitalist system, adopting instead Gomper's business unionism, while the latter belonged to the same "ideological family" as the Knights of Labor, aiming at the establishment of cooperatives for more harmony between capital and labour. Why many Quebec workers opted for secular national unions, given their ideological similarity with the stronger and better-funded international unions, is explained by the presence of "an old nationalist basis" (p. 120), a result of the cultural barrier between French Canada and the rest of the continent which had appeared long before the clergy's intervention. It is worth mentioning that, while Rouillard gave disproportionate attention to the militancy of unionized boot-and-shoe workers in his thesis, he was never concerned about the extremely low rate of strike participation among all boot-and-shoe workers, which frequently amounted to less than fifteen per cent of the workers per establishment.[12] As a matter of fact, both national and international unions advocated the development of small, fragmented craft locals in this industry, based on a few skilled occupations, in a work environment ripe for industrial unionism. But in spite of this reality, and precisely because of its ideological determinism, this book takes its place among the most important volumes in the field.

Finally, Rouillard also wrote a popular synthesis of the CSN's history from 1921 to 1981 (*Histoire de la C.S.N., 1921–1981*, Montreal: Boréal Express 1981). He succeeded in making this book accessible to the general public by including numerous illustrations and historical documents, thus answering the call of those who had been expecting such a work for many years. Although this is not the first history of the CSN,[13] it is the most up-to-date version of what stands out as a very influential institution, particularly during the last two decades. But what is truly amazing about this book is that, although the author is well aware of the relatively small number of wage-earners in Quebec who were actually represented by this federation, he still maintains that "the history of workers first begins by knowing about their union organization" (p. 11), and definitely leaves the impression that this synthesis concerns all Quebec workers. To put matters bluntly, it is actually concerned with the national fraction of unionized wage-earners, that is, at the most, one-quarter of the 5.6 per cent unionized in 1911 (or 1.4 per cent of all wage-earners), one-third of his estimated 16.8 per cent unionized in 1941, and 22.6 per cent of the 31.8 per cent unionized in 1960 (or seven per cent of all wage-earners). [14] How a historical account of an organization representing between 1.4 and 7 per cent of all wage-earners in Quebec can be presented as the starting point for the history of Quebec workers is a type of magic that trade-union studies have performed in the past. It is true that CSN leaders have fought in the recent past for measures and changes that were designed to reform, or even to transform, the whole capitalist system. Even so, one still wonders how influential this federation has been for the huge and silent majority of non-unionized industrial workers, for those who toil in the service industries, for domestic and part-time workers, and for the unemployed, not to mention for those who are represented by other federations.

Fernand Harvey, another member of the new generation of labour historians of the early 1970s, was more innovative in his approach, breaking decidedly with the superstructural tradition. Well aware of the fact that historiography put too much emphasis on the labour movement and unionism, he introduced a sociological framework of analysis which had as its starting point "workers in their work environment." To complement trade-unionism, he turned to the totality of the workers' socio-economic environment: their relations with other classes, their social mobility, their ethnic divisions, and the *question nationale*. [15] This problem was dealt with in his book *Révolution industrielle et travailleurs* (Montreal: Boréal Express 1978), a study of the testimony of Quebec wage-earners, employers, and professionals before the Royal Commission on the Relations of Capital and Labour in the 1880s. At a time when only a few European labour specialists had grasped the importance of the basic structure of labour relations to our understanding of social antagonisms – what has come to be called the labour process – Harvey devoted two chapters of his book to two essential components of this process: technical methods of production and the organization of human activity of labour power. It is true that this testimony was insufficient in itself to draw an exhaustive picture of every work environment and that one is still left with the impression that mechanization was a swift and definitive phenomenon. Yet this study is a remarkable contribution because it links the history of work to the history of workers, and because the author successfully summarizes the structural, functional, and cultural contexts from which this testimony came. Here is a book that will meet the expectations of those who, though well aware of the key role of specific modalities of social relationships of production, want to keep sight of the more general social interactions during the industrial revolution. It should be read in conjunction with Kealey's *Toronto Workers Respond to Industrial Capitalism*.

The growing interest in workers and their workplace is clearly more pronounced among researchers of artisanal or handicraft production in Quebec. Elaborate descriptions of artisans' techniques, shops, tools, and products have been the strength of ethnologists' and ethno-historians' accounts of the material, oral, and written culture of blacksmiths, leather workers, clock makers, and so on.[16] It has been argued, however, that their retrospective approach, based as it is on artifacts, testimonies of aging artisans in remote areas, and folkloric documents, has seldom given a dynamic picture of the social fabric and relations of production at a time when masters, journeymen, and apprentices were the main producers of finished and semi-finished goods. To fulfil this goal, other, more historically minded scholars now rely on notarial archives (such as apprenticeship indentures), judicial records, early newspapers, and censuses to determine the role, status, mutual responsibilities, working conditions, standards of living, and conflicts of these direct producers. Jean-Pierre Hardy and David-Thiery Ruddel's *Les apprentis artisans à Québec 1660–1825* (Montreal: Les presses de l'Université du Québec 1977) remains the most comprehensive publication along those lines.[17] The reader may find their logic to be too inductive and their statements either too obvious or too hypothetical, but one should note the scantiness of the data base, an almost insurmountable handicap for labour specialists studying these early stages of colonial society. Overall, this study of apprenticeship in Quebec City is informative and abundantly illustrated, and fills what would be otherwise an enormous gap in our literature.[18]

Younger historians are presently compiling similar data for the early decades of the nineteenth century, when the data base expands significantly and the transition to the capitalist mode of production begins to take shape. For the emerging generation of academics, the essence of this transitory phenomenon is not sought in the rise of steam-powered factories but in who controls production, in the devalorization of the traditional work processes, and in the increasing appropriation of surplus value by merchants and creditors.[19] Added to this is a growing corpus of literature on the formation of the working class in "peripheral" areas, stretching from the *engagés* in the fur trade, during the seventeenth and eighteenth centuries, to the railroad, mining, forestry, and fishery workers of the nineteenth and twentieth centuries.[20] At last, one can begin to see the day when an exhaustive study of this transition will be brought to completion, incorporating the numerous facets and successive stages of the emergence of capitalism as a dominant mode of production throughout the province. A similar synthesis regarding the impact of monopoly capital upon labour processes and relations, such issues as Taylorism, Fordism, automation, and the uneven relations between monopolist and non-monopolist factions of capital is more unlikely, as only a handful of students have responded so far to the otherwise influential works of writers such as Harry Braverman, Benjamin Coriat, Michel Aglieta, and Nicos Poulantzas.[21]

However important one considers work and the "culture" of the workplace to be to labour studies, labour power cannot be dissociated from the prevailing conditions within which it is reproduced, as was well understood by Herbert B. Ames almost a century ago. Realizing that Montreal's Victorian bourgeoisie knew more about London ghettos, Paris beggars, and New York tenements than about its own proletariat, this son of a prominent shoe manufacturer became a reformer, and compiled an accurate survey of housing costs, population density, health conditions, and death rate in an industrial ward west of the metropolis. Republished in 1972, his book, *The City Below the Hills* (Michael S. Bliss, ed., Toronto: University of Toronto Press), was a great inspiration to Terry Copp, who began a similar survey of the condition of the working class in Montreal between 1897 and 1929. In *The Anatomy of Poverty* (Toronto: McClelland and Stewart 1974),[22] Copp not only extends Ames' survey to the Great Depression and to all wards of Montreal, he further argues that, in the best philanthropic tradition, Ames avoided the real causes of this destitution: wages and working conditions. After surveying such issues as the real income of the working class, women and children in the labour force, access to the education system, housing conditions, public health, welfare, and labour unrest, the author comes to the conclusion that the great prosperity of the early part of the twentieth century was not shared by all Montrealers, as "the conditions of life for the working class population of Montreal improved only very slightly between 1897 and 1929" (p. 140). Subsistence wages remained at the source of this chronic poverty, because Montreal's economy traditionally provided fewer opportunities for skilled workers, and was characterized by a higher level of seasonal unemployment as a result of the severe winters in this part of the continent. Income redistribution was further restricted by a lower level of taxation than in Toronto, as a result of corruption and patronage, and because the city of Montreal, where the lower classes lived and worked, shared the island with independent municipalities which provided the upper classes with a shelter from the cost of basic city services.

Copp's book is not the only source depicting working-class conditions in Quebec. One can always pore through the above-mentioned works of Hamelin, Rouillard, Harvey, Hardy, and Ruddel, and of others who have attempted to make a contribution to this theme.[23] But *The Anatomy of Poverty* was outstanding in its effort to compare Montreal with other industrial cities and to explain why this particular city was such a poor environment for the reproduction of its workforce, even in times of great prosperity.

Nor can labour power be dissociated from the working-class family and its broader socio-cultural environment. The topic of women at work is a complex one, because these individuals are found not only in the labour market but in the household as well. Historians have only recently taken up the challenge of exploring the interaction between family life and women's participation in the labour market.[24] Previous publications on the conditions of women in Quebec either neglected to make such a link or did not favour a class perspective. Thus, one of the most ambitious feminist works – an attempt to rewrite four centuries of Quebec history from the viewpoint of women's contributions – mostly perceived these women as rural or urban beings, transcending their social position on the basis of their "common" sexual subjection and struggle for equality (Le Collectif Clio, *L'Histoire des femmes au Québec depuis quatre siècles*, Montreal: Quinze 1982). Marie Lavigne and Yolande Pinard's work *Travailleuses et féministes: les femmes dans la société québécoise* (Montreal: Boréal Express 1983), is much more informative about working-class women's economic role and social conditions prior to World War II. Uunfortunately, however, the book is essentially interested with work performed outside the household, and, although some chapters are more or less relevant to labour studies, fails to document the most active period of women's participation in the labour market, from the 1940s onward. Moreover, the authors' argument concerning women's oppression in the workplace is not entirely accurate, as it stems from a global societal judgment on sexual discrimination rather than from a rigorous analysis of its manifestations in the social relationships of production.[25] Francine Barry's very rapid survey of women's work from 1940 to 1970 (*Le travail de la femme au Québec*, Montreal: Les presses de l'Université du Québec 1977) may partially fill the second of these deficiencies, but the third one will require a better knowledge of the labour process and the culture of the workplace. As for the first one – the interaction between capital and household labour processes – it is addressed in Bettina Bradbury's model work in which she proposes to bring together labour history, women's history, and the history of the family.[26] In *Maîtresses de maison, maîtresses d'école* (Montreal: Boréal Express 1983), edited by Nadia Fahmy Eid and Micheline Dumont, Bradbury introduces the concept of the "familial economy" of Montreal's working class during the 1870s, shedding light on the role of each family member and on how the family's collective strategy of survival could be adapted to various living conditions. In Joy Parr's *Childhood and Family in Canadian History* (Toronto: McClelland and Stewart 1982), Bradbury discusses the importance of the orphanage for fragmented working-class families struck by death, illness, or the vagaries of the labour market, from 1860 to 1885. She later added further evidence about "non-wage forms of survival," such as raising pigs and cows in the middle of Montreal and keeping boarders.[27] These intricacies of domestic labour during early industrial capitalism were reinforced by "gender-based wage differentials" which hardened "the identification of the home as women's place." Instead of focusing solely on women's involvement in wage labour, as is the case in the above-mentioned work by Lavigne and Pinard, Bradbury's research "highlights both the centrality of women's role in the sphere of reproduction in the home, and their importance as a reserve army of labour."[28]

For information on the activities of workers outside the workplace and the familial economy, one can always turn to numerous articles on "popular culture," assuming, of course, that these recreational events and cultural facilities are as relevant to the typical unskilled worker as they are to other factions of the "lower classes." No key work has been produced as yet, but mention should be made of excellent reports on the culture of one Montreal tavern in the late nineteenth century,[29] on marriage practices in a working-class ward of Montreal in the opening years of this century,[30] on the social stratification of sport,[31] on popular theatres, exhibitions, and circuses, and on the cultural repression by the church during the Victorian and Edwardian periods.[32] Still, very little has been said about the daily culture of the street, the extent and breakdown of deviancy and of the "underground" culture in working-class communities, and the inter-occupational and inter-ethnic relationships within the proletariat. Indicative of these lacunae is a historiographical survey of working class culture in Montreal between 1880 and 1920 (Yvan Lamonde, Lucia Feretti, and Daniel Leblanc, *La culture ouvrière à Montréal*, Quebec City: IQRC 1982), in which the authors define their field along material and institutional parameters, which is an ade-

quate way of establishing in what context these cultural manifestations took place but leaves to the reader's imagination what truly
characterized this culture and its subcultures. Given this lack of a
major work on working-class culture in Quebec, what necessarily
follows is the absence of an in-depth analysis of the impact of "mass
culture" on the traditional values and practices of the proletariat,
even though these new cultural media have already received their
share of attention.[33]

Although there is no absolute certainty that an increasing interest
in ethnic "collectivities" carries with it a reasonably elaborate class
perspective, inter-ethnic relationships and the subcultures of the
working class have been the focus of a handful of authors interested
with the convergence of ethnic and labour studies.[34] If Quebec's
economic development is mostly represented by labour-intensive
industries and low skill requirements for much of its history, then
one should first be concerned with the reserve army of labour whose
roots are found in the immigration of Irish, Italian, and Jewish people, and their interactions with French-Canadian unskilled workers
coming from the countryside. To get a global picture of these interactions and of the ethnic division of labour in Quebec, the reader
will have to rely on scattered contributions which follow roughly
three major immigration waves: the Irish,[35] during the early Victorian
era, the Italians and the Jews,[36] during the first three decades of
this century, and the immigration from the Third World,[37] in more
recent years. After all, knowledge of working-class culture in Quebec, as elsewhere, involves numerous avenues and perspectives,
and, given Quebec's notorious lag in ethnic studies and the superstructural bias of its labour studies, it is hardly surprising that this
cultural experience is just beginning to be reconstituted.

Upon reading these few pages on more innovative labour studies,
one may come to the conclusion that this superstructural bias is no
longer as problematic as it used to be. This is partially true, but the
emphasis here on the more basic social and cultural perspectives is
still a minority position. An uninterrupted flow of published material
continues, adding to our knowledge of labour unions and federations, the ideological influence of the church, and the lack of influence of communism.[38] This literature is worth reviewing, but it
would have been impossible to give a satisfactory account of it here
without sacrificing work on the daily world of the worker or without
giving Quebec labour studies a disproportionate importance in the
Canadian context.

Further inquiry should be directed first to the bibliographical
works already quoted, as well as to an interesting discussion about
the conjunctural background of Quebec labour studies by Fernand

Harvey (*Le mouvement ouvrier au Québec,* Montreal: Boréal Express 1980).

RESOURCES

As one would expect with a burgeoning field, the resources available to researchers have multiplied over the last fifteen years. The most important bibliographic works include R.G. Hann et al., comps., *Primary Sources in Canadian Working-Class History* (Kitchener, Ont.: Dumont 1973); Peter Weinrich, comp., *Social Protest from the Left in Canada, 1870–1970: A Bibliography* (Toronto: University of Toronto Press 1982); Douglas Vaisey, comp., *The Labour Companion: A Bibliography of Canadian Labour History Based on Materials Printed from 1950 to 1975* (Halifax: Committee on Canadian Labour History 1980); and Louis-Marie Tremblay, comp., *Bibliographie des Relations du Travail au Canada, 1940–1967* (Montreal: Les presses de l'Université de Montréal 1969). These bibliographic compendiums are kept up to date by annual bibliographies published in *Labour/Le Travail* and *Relations industrielles.*

Labour/Le Travail is the bi-annual publication of the Committee on Canadian Labour History (CCLH).[39] It began as an annual in 1976, and switched to its current bi-annual format in 1980. In addition to articles, it publishes research reports, research notes, archival notes, review essays, reviews, and book notes. As the organ of the CCLH, it also keeps members informed of the Committee's activities, which include participation in the Internationale Tagung der Arbeiterbewegung (ITH) and the International Association of Labour History Institutions (IALHI). The CCLH has also cooperated in sponsoring a series of international comparative conferences, including Coventry (1980), Wales (1986), and an Australian-Canadian conference in Sydney (1988). In Quebec the CCLH has a companion organization, Le Regroupement des chercheurs-chercheuses en histoire des travailleurs-travailleuses du Québec (RCHTQ), which publishes a *Bulletin.*[40]

Archivists with specific labour interests have recently organized the Canadian Association of Labour Archivists, which publishes a *Newsletter.*[41] Archival materials relating to labour have been listed in Hann et al., *Primary Sources,* and in the ongoing Archive Notes in *Labour/Le Travail.*

Although only briefly noted here, labour studies has established an institutional framework to allow the already solidly established field to develop further in the future. While the politics of the 1980s seem less than propitious for such work, it nevertheless seems certain that the scholarly clock cannot simply be turned back to the refusal of the 1950s and 1960s to deal with questions of labour.

NOTES

1 Contrast Stanley Mealing, "The Concept of Social Class and the Interpretation of Canadian History," *Canadian Historical Review* 46 (1965):
201–18, with the more recent and differing assessments of Kenneth
McNaught, "E.P. Thompson vs. Harold Logan: Writing About Labour
and the Left in the 1970s," *Canadian Historical Review* 57 (1981): 141–68,
and Gregory S. Kealey, "The Writing of Social History in English Canada, 1970–1984," *Social History* 10 (October 1985): 347–65.

2 See David Bercuson's review of *Dreaming of What Might Be* in *Business
History Review* 57 (1983): 589–91.

3 Fernand Ouellet, "La modernisation de l'historiographie et l'émer-
gence de l'histoire sociale," *Recherches sociographiques* 26, no. 1–2
(1985): 40.

4 Gérard Dion, "La recherche en relations industrielles dans les univer-
sités du Québec," in Louis Baudoin, ed., *La recherche au Canada français*
(Montreal: Les presses de l'Université de Montréal 1968), 73 (our
translation).

5 Louis-Marie Tremblay, *Évolution de la philosophie du syndicalisme au Qué-
bec, 1940–1965* (Ottawa: Éditions de l'Université d'Ottawa 1968); Louis
Marie Tremblay, *Le syndicalisme québécois: idéologies de la C.S.N. et de la
F.T.Q., 1940–1970* (Montreal: Les presses de l'Université de Montréal
1972); Jacques Dofny and Paul Bernard, *Le syndicalisme au Québec:
structure et mouvement* (Ottawa: Bureau du Conseil Privé 1968); Paul
Bernard, *Structures et pouvoirs de la Fédération des travailleurs du Québec*
(Ottawa: Bureau du Conseil Privé 1970).

6 Fernand Ouellet, "La modernisation de l'historiographie," 41.

7 Readings on the asbestos strike should include: Pierre Elliott Trudeau,
ed., *La grève de l'amiante* (Montreal: Cité Libre 1958); Hélène David,
"La grève et le bon Dieu: la grève de l'amiante au Québec," in
Fernand Harvey, ed., *Le mouvement ouvrier au Québec* (Montreal: Boréal
Express 1980), 163–84; Jacques Cousineau, S.J., *Réflexions en marge de
"la grève de l'amiante": contribution critique à une recherche* (Montreal: Cahiers de l'Institut social populaire 1958); and Alfred Charpentier's autobiography, *Cinquante ans d'actions ouvrière* (Quebec City: Les presses
de l'Université Laval 1971).

8 First published in French as *Dans le sommeil de nos os* (Montreal: Leméac 1971).

9 One notable exception is H.C. Pentland, "The Lachine Strike of 1843,"
Canadian Historical Review 29, no. 1 (March 1948): 255–77.

10 See also Jean Hamelin, Paul Larocque, and Jacques Rouillard, *Répertoire des grèves dans la province de Québec au XIXe siècle* (Montreal: Les
presses de l'École des Hautes Études Commerciales 1970).

11 Other viewpoints about the militancy of cotton workers are found in Gail Cuthbert-Brandt, "'Weaving-It Together.' Life Cycle and the Industrial Experience of Female Cotton Workers in Quebec," *Labour/Le Travailleur* 7 (Spring 1981): 9–39; Jacques Ferland, "Syndicalisme 'parcellaire' et syndicalisme 'collectif': une interprétation socio-technique des conflits ouvriers dans deux industries québécoises," *Labour/Le Travail* 19 (Spring 1987): 49–88; Jacques Ferland, "When the Cotton Mills 'Girls' Struck for the First Time: A Study of Female Militancy in the Cotton and Boot and Shoe Industries of Quebec (1880–1910)," paper presented at the Canadian Historical Association meetings, Winnipeg, 1986.

12 Jacques Ferland, "Au sujet du syndicalisme 'parcellaire,'" *Labour/Le Travail* 19 (Spring 1987).

13 Others include Alfred Charpentier, *Montée triomphante de la C.T.C.C. de 1921 à 1951* (Montreal: Therien Frères 1951); J. Francoeur, J.-P. Lefebvre, P. Vadeboncoeur, and J.-L. Roux, *En grève! L'histoire de la C.S.N. et des luttes menées par ses militants de 1937 à 1963* (Montreal: Les Éditions du Jour 1963).

14 Estimates taken from Jacques Rouillard, "Le militantisme des travailleurs au Québec et en Ontario (1900–1980): niveau de syndicalisation et mouvement de grève," *Revue d'histoire de l'Amérique française* 37, no. 2 (September 1983): 201–25.

15 Fernand Harvey, "Les travailleurs québécois au xixe siècle: essai d'un cadre d'analyse sociologique," *Revue d'histoire de l'Amérique française* 25, no. 4 (March 1972): 548.

16 A good starting point for this literature is an article by Helene Espesset, Jean-Pierre Hardy, and David-Thiery Ruddel, "Le monde du travail au Québec au xviiie et au xixe siècles: historiographie et état de la question," *Revue d'histoire de l'Amérique française* 25, no. 4 (March 1972): 499–539. Recent publications in ethno-history include: Jean-Claude Dupont, *L'artisan forgeron* (Quebec City: Les presses de l'Université Laval/Éditeur officiel du Québec 1979); Jean-Claude Dupont and Jacques Mathieu, eds., *Les métiers du cuir* (Quebec City: Les presses de l'Université Laval, 1981); Yvan Fortier, *Menuisier-charpentier, artisan du bois de l'ère industrielle* (Montreal: Boréal Express/Musée National de l'Homme 1980). Numerous other similar studies have been sponsored by the Ministère des Affaires culturelles du Québec (direction patrimoine), the National Museum of Man, in Ottawa, and Parks Canada.

17 Peter Moogk has also contributed significantly to our knowledge of artisans in New France, but his published opus remains more scattered: Peter Moogk, "Apprenticeship Indentures: A Key to Artisan Life in New France," *Canadian Historical Association Annual Report* (1971): 65–83; Peter Moogk, "The Ancestor of Quebec's Craft Unions: The Mon-

treal Shoemakers' Protest of 1729," *Histoire des travailleurs québécois: Bulletin du Regroupement des chercheurs-chercheuses en histoire des travailleurs et travailleuses du Québec* 5, no. 1 (1978): 34–9; Peter Moogk, "In the Darkness of a Basement: Craftmen's Associations in Early French Canada," *Canadian Historical Review* 57, no. 4 (1976): 399–439. Maryse Thivierge also contributed a valuable chapter on artisans in *Les métiers du cuir* (see note 16) entitled "Les artisans du cuir au temps de la Nouvelle-France, Québec, 1660–1760," 9–78.

18 This is not to deny the importance of previously published works on the society and relations of production in New France, such as Louise Dechêne, *Habitants et marchands de Montréal au xviiᵉ siècle* (Paris/Montreal: Plon 1974); and Jean Hamelin, *Économie et société en Nouvelle-France* (Quebec City: Les presses de l'Université Laval 1961).

19 During the 1970s, Quebec historians mostly associated this transition with an elaborate manufacturing division of labour and with the rise of factories, beginning around 1850. See Paul-André Linteau, René Durocher, and Jean-Claude Robert, *Histoire du Québec contemporain* (Montreal: Boréal Express 1979), 141; and Joanne Burgess, "L'industrie de la chaussure à Montréal (1840–1870). Le passage de l'artisanal à la fabrique," *Revue d'histoire de l'Amérique française* 31, no. 2 (September 1977): 187–210. But earlier changes within the artisanal mode of production are presently being sought in previous decades, with the help of thousands of deeds. See Robert Sweeny, "Financing the transition in a colonial city: Montréal 1820–1828," *Protesting History* (Montreal: Montreal Business History Project 1982–84); and Robert Tremblay, "La formation matérielle de la classe ouvrière à Montréal entre 1790 et 1830," *Revue d'histoire de l'Amérique française* 33 (1979) 39–50.

20 Alan Greer, "Fur trade labour and Lower Canadian agrarian structure," *Canadian Historical Association Annual Report* (1981): 197–214; R.C. Harris, "Of Poverty and Helplessness in Petite-Nation," *Canadian Historical Review* 52 (1971): 23–50; Normand Séguin, *La conquête du sol au 19e siècle* (Montreal: Boréal Express 1977); Camille Legendre, "Les débuts de la rémunération à la pièce dans l'industrie forestière," *Recherches sociographiques* 20, no. 3 (September-October 1979): 301–35; Jean-Pierre Kesteman, "Les travailleurs de la construction de chemins de fer dans la région de Sherbrooke (1851–1853)," *Revue d'histoire de l'Amérique française* 31, no. 4 (March 1978): 525–46; Jose E. Igartua et Marine de Freminville, "Les origines des travailleurs de l'Alcan au Saguenay, 1925–1939," *Revue d'histoire de l'Amérique française* 37, no. 2 (September 1983): 291–308.

21 Robert Nahuet, "Une expérience canadienne de taylorisme: le cas des usines Angus du Canadien Pacifique," M.A. thesis, Université du Québec à Montréal, Montreal, 1984; Paul-André Lapointe, "Régulation et crise du rapport salarial fordiste aux usines Jonquière de l'Alcan,

1943–1981," M.A. thesis, Université du Québec à Montréal, Montreal, 1985; Jacques Ferland, "Évolution des rapports sociaux dans l'industrie canadienne du cuir au tournant du 20ᵉ siècle," Ph.D. thesis, McGill University, Montreal, 1985.

22 Also translated into French and published as *Classe ouvrière et pauvreté: les conditions de vie des travailleurs montréalais 1897–1929* (Montreal: Boréal Express 1978).

23 Paul Larocque, "Aperçu sur la condition ouvrière à Québec, 1896–1914," *Labour/Le travailleur* 1 (1976): 122–38; Jean de Bonville, *Jean-Baptiste Gagnepetit: les travailleurs montréalais à la fin du 19e siècle* (Montreal: Aurore 1975); J. Saint-Pierre, "Le quartier Saint-Roch de Québec: l'environnement socio-économique des travailleurs, 1941–1971," M.A. thesis, Laval University, Quebec City, 1974; Nicole Thivierge, "La condition sociale des ouvriers de l'industrie de la chaussure à Québec, 1900–1940," in *Les métiers du cuir*, 371–413 (see note 16).

24 Colloque UQAM-Regroupement des chercheurs-chercheuses en histoire des travailleurs et travailleuses du Québec, "Histoire des travailleurs/ histoire des femmes: points de rencontre et points de rupture," *Bulletin du Regroupement des chercheurs-chercheuses en histoire des travailleurs et travailleuses du Québec* 32–33, no. 11 (Summer–Fall 1985): 18–114.

25 Yolande Cohen, "Femmes et histoire," *Recherches sociographiques* 25, no. 3 (September–December 1984): 470.

26 "Commentaires de B. Bradbury sur l'histoire des travailleurs, des femmes et de la famille," *Bulletin du Regroupement des chercheurs-chercheuses en histoire des travailleurs et travailleuses du Québec* 32–33, no. 11 (Summer–Fall 1985): 77.

27 B. Bradbury, "Pigs, Cows and Boarders: Non-Wage Forms of Survival Among Montreal Families, 1861–1891," *Labour/Le Travail* 14 (Fall 1984): 9–46.

28 B. Bradbury, "Women and Wage Labour in a Period of Transition: Montreal, 1861–1881," *Histoire sociale/Social History* 17 (May 1984): 115–32, quoted 116.

29 Peter DeLottinville, "Joe Beef of Montreal: Working-Class Culture and the Tavern, 1869–1889," *Labour/Le Travailleur* 8/9 (Fall 1981/Spring 1982): 9–40.

30 Lucia Ferretti, "Marriage et cadre de vie familiale dans une paroisse ouvrière montréalaise: Sainte-Brigide, 1900–1914," *Revue d'histoire de l'Amérique française* 39, no. 2 (Fall 1985): 233–53.

31 Alan Metcalfe, "Working-Class Physical Recreation in Montreal, 1860–1895," *Working Papers in the Sociological Study of Sport and Leisure* 1, no. 2 (1978); A. Metcalfe, "Organized Sport and Social Stratification in Montreal, 1840–1901," in R.S. Gruneau and J.G. Albinson, eds., *Canadian Sport. Sociological Perspectives* (Don Mills, Ont.: Addison-Wesley 1976).

32 Groupe de recherche en art populaire, *Travaux et conférences 1975–1979* (Montreal: Département d'histoire de l'art, Université du Québec à Montréal 1979).

33 See, for instance, Yvan Lamonde and Pierre-François Hébert, *Le cinéma au Québec: essai de statistique historique (1896 à nos jours)* (Québec City: Institut québécois de recherche sur la culture [IQRC] 1981).

34 A summary of these is found in Gary Caldwell, *Les études ethniques au Québec* (Quebec City: IQRC 1983), and, for the Jewish workers, in David Rome, Judith Nefsky, and Paule Obermeir, *Les Juifs au Québec* (Quebec City: IQRC 1981). See also Bruno Ramirez, "La recherche sur les italiens du Québec," *Questions de culture* 2 (1982): 103–12.

35 H.C. Pentland, "The Lachine Strike," *Canadian Historical Review* (September 1948): 255–77; G.R.C. Keep, "Irish Adjustment in Montreal, 1847–1867," *Canadian Historical Review* 31, no. 1 (March 1950): 39–46; Raymond Boily, *Les Irlandais et le canal de Lachine: la grève de 1843* (Montreal: Leméac 1980); Herman Van Omnen, "Labour Riots in Quebec 1857–1879," *The Register (McGill History Journal)* 1, no. 1 (March 1980): 50–67.

36 Evelyn Dumas, *Dans le sommeil de nos os* (Montreal: Leméac 1971); David Rome, *On Our Forerunners at Work* (Montreal: Canadian Jewish Congress, Coll. Canadian Jewish Archives, New Series, no. 9, 1978); Bruno Ramirez and Michael Balso, *The Italians of Montreal: from sojourning to settlement, 1900–1921* (Montreal: Les Éditions du Courant 1980); B. Ramirez, *Les premiers Italiens de Montréal. L'origine de la Petite Italie du Québec* (Montreal: Boréal Express 1984); Robert Harney, "Montreal's King of Italian Labour: A Case Study of Padronism," *Labour/Le Travailleur* 4 (1979): 57–84; Roberto Perin, "Conflits d'identité et d'allégeance: la propagande du Consulat Italien de Montréal dans les années 1930," *Questions de culture* 2 (1982): 81–102.

37 Among others: Joseph Kage, *A Brief Account of the Admission of Jewish Immigrants from North Africa* (Montreal: JIAS 1974); Paul Dejean, *Les Haitiens du Québec* (Montreal: Les presses de l'Université du Québec 1978); Ban Seng Hoe, "Folk-tales and Social Structure: The Case of the Chinese in Montreal," *Canadian Folklore Canadien* 1, no. 1–2 (1979); Jean-Pierre Gosselin, "Une immigration de la onzième heure: les Latino-Américains," *Recherches sociographiques* 25, no. 3 (September–December 1984): 391–420; Stephanos Constantinides, *Les Grecs du Québec* (Montreal: O'Metoikos/Le Métèque 1983). One notable exception to this chronological distribution of ethnic studies is Denise Helly, "Les buandiers chinois de Montréal au tournant du siècle," *Recherches sociographiques* 25, no. 3 (September–December 1984): 343–65.

38 François Cyr and Rémi Roy, *Éléments d'histoire de la F.T.Q. La F.T.Q. et la question nationale* (Montreal: Édition coopérative Albert St. Martin 1981); Louise Clermont-Laliberté, *Dix ans de pratiques syndicales, la*

C.E.Q. 1970–1980 (Sainte-Foy: Centrale de l'enseignement du Québec 1981); Jean Gérin-Lajoie, *Les Métallos 1936–1981* (Montreal: Boréal Express 1982); Fernand Dumont, Jean Hamelin, and Jean-Paul Montminy, eds., *Idéologies au Canada français 1940–1976. Tome II: Les mouvements sociaux. Les syndicats* (Québec: Les presses de l'Université Laval 1981); Léo Roback and Louis-Marie Tremblay, *Le nationalisme au sein des syndicats québécois* (Montreal: École des relations industrielles 1979); CSN/CEQ, *Histoire du mouvement ouvrier au Québec (1825–1976)* (Montreal: CSN/CEQ 1979); Jean Boivin, *The Evolution of Bargaining Power in the Province of Québec Public Sector* (Quebec City: Les presses de l'Université Laval 1980); Robert Parise, *Le fondateur du syndicalisme catholique au Québec, Mgr. Eugène Lapointe: sa pensée et son action syndicale* (Montreal: Les presses de l'Université du Québec 1978); Jacques Cousineau, s.j., *L'Église d'ici et le social: 1940–1960. 1. La commission sacerdotale d'Études sociales* (Montreal: Bellarmin 1982); Robert Comeau and Bernard Dionne, *Les communistes au Québec 1936–1956* (Montreal: Presses de l'unité 1980); Andrée Lévesque, *Virage à gauche interdit. Les communistes, les socialistes et leurs ennemis au Québec, 1929–1939* (Montreal: Boréal Express 1984).

39 *Labour/Le Travail* and Committee on Canadian Labour History, History Department, Memorial University of Newfoundland, St. John's, Newfoundland, A1C 5S7.

40 Département d'histoire, Université du Québec à Montréal, CP 8888, Succursale A, Montréal, Québec, H3C 3P8.

41 c/o NA, 395 Wellington Street, Ottawa, Ontario, K1A 0N3.

LIST OF TWENTY-FIVE MOST IMPORTANT BOOKS IN LABOUR STUDIES

Abella, Irving. *Nationalism Communism and Canadian Labour: The C.I.Q., the Communist Party of Canada and the Canadian Congress of Labour, 1935–1956.* Toronto: University of Toronto Press 1973.

Armstrong, Hugh and Pat Armstrong. *The Double Ghetto: Canadian Women and their Segregated Work.* Toronto: McClelland and Stewart 1987.

Avery, Donald. *"Dangerous Foreigners": European Immigrant Workers and Labour Radicalism in Canada, 1896–1932.* Toronto: McClelland and Stewart 1979.

Babcock, Robert. *Gompers in Canada: A Study of American Continentalism Before the First World War.* Toronto: University of Toronto Press 1974.

Bercuson, David. *Confrontation at Winnipeg: Labour, Industrial Relations and the General Strike.* Montreal: McGill-Queen's University Press 1974.

Copp, Terry. *The Anatomy of Poverty: The Condition of the Working Class in Montreal, 1897–1929.* Toronto: McClelland and Stewart 1974.

Craven, Paul. *An Impartial Umpire: Industrial Relations and the Canadian State, 1900–1911.* Toronto: University of Toronto Press 1980.

Forsey, Eugene. *Trade Unions in Canada 1812–1902.* Toronto: University of Toronto Press 1981.

Harvey, Fernand. *Révolution industrielle et travailleurs: une enquête sur les rapports entre le capital et le travail au Québec à la fin du 19ᵉ siècle.* Montreal: Boréal Express 1978.

Heron, Craig and Robert Storey, eds. *On the Job: Confronting the Labour Process in Canada.* Montreal: McGill-Queen's University Press 1986.

Kealey, Gregory S. *Toronto Workers Respond to Industrial Capitalism, 1862–1892.* Toronto: University of Toronto Press 1980.

Kealey, Gregory S. and Bryan D. Palmer. *Dreaming of What Might Be: The Knights of Labor in Ontario, 1880–1900.* New York: Cambridge University Press 1982.

Luxton, Meg. *More Than a Labour of Love: Three Generations of Women's Work in the Home.* Toronto: Women's Press 1980.

McCormack, Andrew Ross. *Reformers, Rebels and Revolutionaries: The Western Canadian Radical Movement, 1899–1919.* Toronto: University of Toronto Press 1977.

MacDowell, Laurel Sefton. *Remember Kirkland Lake: The History and Effects of the Kirkland Lake Goldminers' Strike, 1941–42.* Toronto: University of Toronto Press 1983.

Morton, Desmond. *Working People.* Ottawa: Deneau & Greenberg 1980.

Palmer, Bryan D. *The Character of Class Struggle: Essays in Canadian Working Class History 1850–1985.* Toronto: McClelland and Stewart 1986.

– *A Culture in Conflict: Skilled Workers and Industrial Capitalism in Hamilton, Ontario, 1860–1914.* Montreal: McGill-Queen's University Press 1979.

– *Working-Class Experience: The Rise and Reconstitution of Canadian Labour, 1800–1980.* Toronto: University of Toronto Press 1983.

Pentland, H. Clare. *Labour and Capital in Canada, 1650–1860.* Toronto: J. Lorimer 1981.

Phillips, Erin and Paul Phillips. *Women at Work: Inequality in the Labour Market.* Toronto: J. Lorimer 1983.

Rinehart, James. *The Tyranny of Work.* Second edition. Toronto: Harcourt Brace Jovanovich Canada 1987.

Rouillard, Jacques. *Histoire de la CSN, 1921–1981.* Montreal: Boréal Express 1981.

– *Les Syndicats nationaux au Québec de 1900 à 1930.* Quebec City: Les presses de l'Université Laval 1979.

– *Les travailleurs du coton au Québec, 1900–1915.* Montreal: Les presses de l'Université du Québec 1974.

CHAPTER THREE

Religious Studies

BY GUY LAPERRIÈRE AND
WILLIAM WESTFALL

INTRODUCTION: RELIGION AND CANADA

Religion has held a central place in Canada's development. While its activities have taken a variety of forms, the dominant roles have been played by the major churches and the new religious groups that have arisen throughout the nation's history. However, this opening statement cannot hide the fact that religious matters fell into the background during the late 1960s and early 1970s as a result of the general trend in secularization which swept Canada and the Western world in that period. The results of this trend are well known: decreased attendance at religious services, departures and a diminishing number of vocations among priests, brothers, and nuns, the weakening of moral precepts and a trend to the freedom of morals, an increase in civil weddings and in divorce, and the silence of religious authorities.

This decline in the traditional churches is reflected in the decennial statistics, as shown in table 1.

This table reflects the fall of established Protestant churches, the arrival of certain immigrant groups (Greek, Muslim), the rise in certain religious groups (Pentecostals, Mormons), and, above all, the progress of religious indifference.

In the mid-1970s, however, the general trend changed and the religious phenomenon manifested itself once again in a number of ways, upon occasion giving rise to heated debate. The rise of feminism during the same period challenged many of the church's precepts. Already, in 1968, Pope Paul VI's encyclical *Humanae Vitae* forbidding contraception had done much to discredit the Catholic

Table 1
Religious Denominations in Canada, 1971–1981

Denomination	1971 (% of total)	1981 (% of total)	Change in %
Roman Catholics	9,975,000 (46.2%)	11,212,000 (46.6%)	+0.4%
United Church	3,769,000 (17.5%)	3,758,000 (15.6%)	-1.9%
Anglicans	2,543,000 (11.8%)	2,436,000 (10.1%)	-1.7%
Presbyterians	872,000 (4.0%)	812,000 (3.4%)	-0.6%
Lutherans	716,000 (3.3%)	703,000 (2.9%)	-0.4%
Baptists	667,000 (3.1%)	697,000 (2.9%)	-0.2%
Eastern Orthodox	317,000 (1.5%)	362,000 (1.5%)	--
Pentecostals	220,000 (1.0%)	339,000 (1.4%)	+0.4%
Jews	276,000 (1.3%)	296,000 (1.2%)	-0.1%
Ukranian Catholics	228,000 (1.1%)	191,000 (0.8%)	-0.3%
Mennonites	168,000 (0.8%)	189,000 (0.8%)	
Jehovah's Witnesses	175,000 (0.8%)	143,000 (0.6%)	-0.2%
Salvation Army	120,000 (0.6%)	125,000 (0.5%)	-0.1%
Muslims	--	98,000 (0.4%)	+0.4%
Mormons	67,000 (0.3%)	90,000 (0.4%)	+0.1%
No religion/ No religious preference	930,000 (4.3%)	1,784,000 (7.4%)	+3.1%
Total population	21,568,000	24,083,000	

Source: *Census of Canada*, 1971, 1981

church in the eyes of liberals and a majority of couples. The opposition of established churches to divorce and abortion did not prevent Parliament from passing legislation liberalizing both. Abortion clinics set up by Dr. Henry Morgentaler in Montreal, Toronto, and Winnipeg brought him before the courts and sparked a series of demonstrations, by both the "free choice" and the "pro-life" movements. The play *Les fées ont soif,* by Denise Boucher, which dealt with the role of the Catholic church in the secular alienation of women, was the cause of much controversy in Quebec, with, once again, a number of demonstrations taking place for and against.[1] Within the churches themselves, women demanded equality and called for the right to have access to ordained ministries. This movement created particular dissension within the Anglican church, which finally consented to the ordainment of women on November 30, 1976.

Elsewhere, influenced no doubt by the strong positions taken by their American counterparts, the religious authorities of the principal Canadian denominations began to take stands on social and political issues in addition to moral ones. There was much debate in January, 1983, when Catholic bishops opposed the economic policy of the Trudeau government. Other causes are vigorously promoted by the churches: disarmament, peace, the fight against poverty, the promotion of the family, the defence of native peoples.

Last, but not least, the revival of religious sentiment made itself felt through the proliferation of what were called "the new religions." Pentecostals, charismatics, and apostles of Eastern religions attracted a growing number of followers, to the detriment of the traditional churches. This rise in religious sentiment – while secularization continued to progress concomitantly – came to a climax in September, 1984, while Pope John Paul II was on a twelve-day visit to Canada, and made people aware of the multitude of forms of religious commitment in the various regions of the country.

It is interesting to follow the production of studies and research on the religious development of Canada and its present-day situation that developed in parallel to this general movement of ebb followed by partial resurgence of religion. Here, too, one finds an interesting and perhaps curious pattern. The study of religion, which once was so central to Canadian academic life, fell upon hard times as traditional religious forms lost their authority in Canadian society as a whole. Recently, however, the study of religion has enjoyed a rebirth, although now scholars, much like those who worship God, approach the deity in new ways, often from outside of the traditional denominational and ecclesiastical frameworks that have shaped the study of religion in Canada in the past.

A brief examination of the forces that have helped to define this pattern explains in part why scholars have done certain types of work (and not other types), and also provides a general commentary upon the changing place of religion within Canadian life. At one time religion was at the very heart of Canadian society. During the nineteenth century, for example, religion deeply coloured the way in which people understood the world itself. Religion was over-reaching and synthetic; it provided the very categories for organizing time and place, and yet, in the eyes of contemporaries, it was able to transcend the limitations that such categories imposed. Religion seemed like the eternal sun around which all else must revolve. At this time the study of religion was at the very centre of academic life in Canada. Almost all institutions of higher learning constructed their curricula around the study of religion and religiously related subjects, so that students would receive a general synthesis of knowledge and understand the relationship between the structure of the world, the course of human history, and God's plan.

By the middle of the twentieth century, religion had fallen dra-matically from this exalted position. Many of the events that marked this decline are quite well known. Church attendance (especially for the major Protestant groups) declined; the moral attitudes that were so much a part of nineteenth-century religious life no longer exer-cised the quasi-legal authority they once enjoyed; the state replaced the church in many aspects of social life, such as education and health care; and, at a more basic level, new concepts of knowledge and the self seemed to remove both time and place from sacred control – or, worse still, to place them under the authority of a supreme force that worked according to decidedly un-Christian prin-ciples. As a part of this process, the study of religion lost its central place in Canadian academic life. The metaphors for interpreting the character of Canada relied upon more measurable phenomena such as the environment, social class, and the impact of a variety of staple products. Knowledge lost the sense of unity that the sacred had provided, and the study of Canada retreated into a number of dis-crete disciplines in which religion played only a minor role.

The study of religion in Canada, however, did not disappear com-pletely; rather, it split along two rather different lines. The com-partmentalization of knowledge gave religion its own proper sphere, and, like so many other segments of knowledge, religion became tied to a professional endeavour. It was reserved for students of theology who might find it useful for a certain type of career. Con-sequently, a good deal of the study of religion in Canada took place within religious institutions as a part of programs of clerical training. For this reason, denominational and institutional studies have dom-inated the field, and even a good deal of the most recent work in religious studies still reflects this traditional ethos.

When religion tried to move outside its own sphere it faced a number of problems. The mainstream of academic life was becoming almost aggressively secularist. It did not acknowledge the formative role of religious belief, and pushed religion to the margin of social analysis. If religion entered the narrative of Canadian development, it did so as a dependent variable that might enrich the structure that sociology, politics, and economics had created. Religion was a guest in someone else's house and had to conform to the terms set down by its host. Consequently, the study of religion outside the traditional institutional framework has tended to cluster around a specific set of political and social themes in which religion has seemed to touch most directly the secular structure of Canadian development.

Only in the last decade has religion begun to break out of this pattern. The growing interest in interdisciplinary and multidisciplinary work which has given rise to such initiatives as Canadian studies, women's studies, and urban studies has provided an academic context that is singularly more helpful for the study of religion. The creation of religious-studies programs and departments that are at least slightly removed from denominational control and exclusively ministerial concerns has also opened up the study of religion, although the subject of religion in Canada still remains for them only a minor focus of scholarly interest. In addition, the growth within the traditional disciplines of such areas as social history and cultural studies has aided the study of religion.

This bibliographical survey is intended to serve as a general guide to the study of Canada within the broad field of religious studies. Designed for the reader who is not conversant with the field and wishes to approach the study of religion and Canada in a reasonably systematic manner, the essay attempts to highlight and comment upon the most important work that has been done in a number of different areas, especially in the last twenty-five years. It does not pretend to be exhaustive, and tends to focus upon the most accessible materials. It also reflects the fact that both of the authors are historians. For a guide to more detailed studies, unpublished graduate material, and a fuller account of the article literature, readers should consult the section on bibliographical sources that introduces this essay and the bibliographical references that appear at the appropriate points in the various sections of the text. One should also consult the other essays in this collection for material that relates to religious themes and issues.

PUBLISHING

The churches are sufficiently established forces within Canadian society to have at their disposal an extensive network which enables them to deliver their message. Although we are limiting ourselves here to the world of research and scholarly publishing, we should first mention the existence of publishers which, at least in the beginning, were religiously oriented. In English Canada, there are very few publishers that are devoted to the scholarly study of religion. With the absorption of Ryerson Press by McGraw-Hill, English Canada lost the one major publisher that produced work in the field. Now works on religion appear occasionally on the lists of publishers who focus primarily on other themes and issues. Of particular note, however, are Wilfrid Laurier University Press and McGill-Queen's University Press, which have shown particular interest in publishing books that deal with religion in Canada. The same development has taken place in Quebec, where we now find works dealing with religion within most of the major publishing companies, which does not prevent the companies founded by religious communities – Fides, Bellarmin, and Éditions Paulines – from continuing to favour the religious field. With prestigious collections such as *Héritage et Projet* (Fides) and *Recherches* (Bellarmin), scholarly publishing is well served. Éditions Paulines concerns itself mainly with popularization, often of superior quality. Fides and Bellarmin also publish works of a popularized nature.

Scholarly journals represent perhaps the major source for recent work of the study of religion in English Canada. Certain denominational journals publish important work, including the *Bulletin of the United Church Archives*, the *Journal of the Canadian Church Historical Society*, and the *Study Sessions of the Canadian Catholic Historical Association/Sessions d'étude de la Société canadienne d'histoire de l'Église catholique*. Of a more general nature are *Studies in Religion/Sciences Religieuses* (*SR*) and, more recently, the *Toronto Journal of Theology*. Issues of the *Canadian Journal of Theology*, which was succeeded by *Studies in Religion* in 1971, also contain important Canadian material. The new interest in religious studies has also led to the appearance of religious material in scholarly journals that are devoted primarily to non-religious concerns. If one reads, for example, recent issues of *Acadiensis*, *The Journal of Canadian Studies*, *Ontario History*, *Social History/Histoire sociale*, la *Revue d'histoire de l'Amérique française*, *Recherches sociographiques*, or the *Canadian Historical Review*, one can find articles about religion that encourage a sense of optimism about the study of religion in the future. In the field of theology, there are the *Laval théologique et philosophique* (published since 1945), which has enjoyed renewed success the last ten years, and the journal of the Montreal Jesuit faculties, *Science et Esprit* (published since 1948). Both publications deal as much with philosophy as they do with theology.

St. Paul's University, in Ottawa, publishes *Église et théologie* (published since 1970) and *Studia Canonica* (published since 1967).

Some of these journals include specialized bibliographies, notably the Canadian Catholic Historical Association's *Study Sessions,* which publishes an annual bibliography of Canadian church history. For the rest, sociologists have been the main workers in the preparation of bibliographical or methodological syntheses on the place of religion in Canadian society. In 1974, Stewart Crysdale and Jean-Paul Montminy presented a bilingual analytical guide, *Religion au Canada/ Religion in Canada* (Quebec City: Les presses de l'Université Laval 1974), which covered for the most part works of a sociological or anthropological nature. Four articles contain valuable bibliographical materials and also address important methodological concerns. N.K. Clifford discusses different ways in which English-Canadian scholars have addressed the relationship between religion and the development of Canadian society ("Religion and the Development of Canadian Society. An Historiographical Analysis," *Church History* 38 (1969): 506–23); Roger O'Toole comments on the work that has been done on the changing role of religion in Canadian culture ("Society, the Sacred and the Secular: Sociological Observations on the Changing Role of Religion in Canadian Culture," in William Westfall, Louis Rousseau, Fernand Harvey, and John Simpson, eds, *Religion/Culture: Comparative Canadian Studies,* Ottawa: Association for Canadian Studies 1985, 99–117). Louis Rousseau has published a valuable essay (in English) on the study of religion in French America ("Religion in French America," *Religious Studies Review* 10 (January 1984): 33–46), and Terrence Murphy reviews in a thorough and critical manner the state of religious history in Atlantic Canada ("The Religious History of Atlantic Canada: the State of the Art," *Acadiensis* 15 (Autumn 1985): 152–74).

Lastly, we can mention the existence of a certain number of learned societies devoted to the study of aspects of religious phenomena. In English Canada almost every religious body has its own association, which works very hard with very limited support to promote the study of religion within its own religious tradition. Two groups are more broadly based. The Canadian Society of Church History tries to draw together a range of scholars who are interested in the history of Canadian religion, while the Canadian Society for the Study of Religion (CSSR) brings together Canadian scholars who are interested in religion as a more general phenomenon. The former is almost exclusively historical in orientation and Canadian in focus, while the latter tends to be multidisciplinary in approach and non-national in character, but occasionally addresses Canadian issues.

Francophones gather within Catholic associations. Among the most important of these are the Association catholique des études bibliques au Canada (ACEBAC), which, with the Société catholique de la Bible (SOCABI), published a remarkable translation of the Gospels (1982), and the Société canadienne de théologie (SCT), which has provided an increasingly lively forum during its annual thematic conferences, whose proceedings are published in the *Héritage et Projet* series. However, it is still within the general journals of history, sociology, anthropology, regional studies, and other human sciences that we often find the most significant articles on religion, beyond the old denominational routes.

OVERVIEWS AND DENOMINATIONAL STUDIES

Until recently, there have been few attempts to provide a general overview of either the history of religion in Canada or the place of religion in Canadian society and culture. In 1956, H.H. Walsh attempted to bring together a host of diverse themes and materials in his book *The Christian Church in Canada* (Toronto: Ryerson). About ten years later, a more ambitious attempt to achieve a general synthesis was made in the three-volume series *The History of the Christian Church in Canada*, edited by John Webster Grant.[2] All of the volumes are historical in structure and institutional in focus; the second and third volumes contain short and very useful bibliographical sections. A collection of essays, *The Churches and the Canadian Experience* (Toronto: Ryerson 1963), also edited by Grant, maintains this denominational and institutional structure. One of the few other general studies is a fine comparative study of the religious history of Canada and the United States by Robert T. Handy, *A History of the Churches in the United States and Canada* (New York: Oxford 1976).

Over the last few years, a number of works have taken a new approach to the general question of religion in Canada. These works tend to be comparative and interdisciplinary; they set out to bring together recent work in both French and English Canada, rather than attempting to realize a single all-encompassing narrative. Stewart Crysdale and Les Wheatcroft have prepared a collection of essays, entitled *Religion in Canadian Society* (Toronto: Macmillan 1976), that contains sections on history and religion in contemporary life as well as a valuable introduction on theory and method. Peter Slater has edited an important collection, *Religion and Culture in Canada* (Waterloo, Ont.: Canadian Corporation for Studies in Religion 1977), which brings together new work by scholars in both French and English Canada. In 1985, the Association for Canadian Studies published a large and ambitious collection of new essays entitled *Religion/Culture: Comparative Canadian Studies* (Ottawa: Association for Canadian Studies 1985). Of the twenty-four papers, ten are in French; the collection addresses such diverse themes as messianism, new religious movements, women and religion, and religion and the arts. In 1983, the Canadian Catholic Historical Society published a collection of essays entitled *Bilan de l'histoire religieuse au Canada/Canadian Catholic History: A Survey* to mark its fiftieth anniversary. This volume presents a good picture of several important areas of historical research: hierarchy and clergy, education, spirituality, missions, politics, and the church and nationality.

Given the limited nature of these general works, one must turn to studies of specific religious groups in order to deepen one's understanding of religion in Canada. Here one finds a long tradition of scholarship; indeed, the churches still provide the focus for a good deal of work that is currently being done in the field. So much is this the case that one must be rather selective, and this commentary serves as a general guide rather than an exhaustive compilation of materials.

The principal works on Catholicism concern Quebec. Upon the occasion of Pope John Paul II's visit to Canada, the Musée du Québec prepared an exhibit entitled *L'Église catholique et la société du Québec* under the direction of Jean Simard (Quebec City: Musée du Québec 1984). Organized in two parts, the work shows the entrenchment of the church in Quebec, and its influence via the mission on native peoples (seventeenth and eighteenth centuries), North America (nineteenth century), and the entire world (twentieth century). If one overlooks its triumphalist side, this abundantly illustrated synthesis constitutes an excellent introduction to the religious history of Quebec.

The most considerable venture in the field, however, is *L'Histoire du catholicisme québécois*, edited by Nive Voisine. Volume 3, on the twentieth century, launched the series with a flourish (Montreal: Boréal Express 1984). This synthesis, more than nine hundred pages long, is the fruit of a collaboration between historian Jean Hamelin and sociologist Nicole Gagnon for Part One (1898–1940), and a more personal synthesis on Hamelin's part for Part Two (from 1940 to the 1980s). This work far exceeds the compilation of existing studies, and is based upon an extensive search of episcopal archives, which is quite exceptional for the religious funds of the twentieth century. It is to be hoped that the other volumes will be out by the end of the decade, which would be remarkable for a project of this scale.

Lastly, there is a somewhat less recent synthesis entitled *Sciences sociales et Églises* (P. Stryckman and J.-P. Rouleau, eds., Montreal:

Bellarmin 1980). Some twenty essays, produced mainly by sociologists but also by theologians and religiologists, present epistemological reflections or research in progress. This volume was the swan song of the Centre de recherches en sociologie religieuse, which at that time (1978) was celebrating its twentieth anniversary and which would give way in 1980 to an enlarged group in religious sciences, which has since published extensively. *Religion et culture au Québec. Figures contemporaines du sacré* (Montreal: Fides 1986), a collection directed by Y. Desrosiers, has been published by a group based in Montréal.

Regrettably, there is no general study in English of the Roman Catholic church in Canada. One must therefore turn to more specific studies, such as Cornelius Jaenen's work on the church in New France (*The Role of the Church in New France*, Toronto: McGraw-Hill Ryerson 1976), A.A. Johnston's study of the church in Nova Scotia (*A History of the Catholic Church in Eastern Nova Scotia*, Antigonish: St. Francis Xavier University Press 1960), Luca Codignola's history of early Catholic colonies in Newfoundland (*The Coldest Harbour of the Land: Simon Stack and Lord Baltimore's Colony in Newfoundland, 1621–1649*, Montreal: McGill-Queen's University Press 1988), and an older study of rather limited use by A.G. Morice on the history of the church in the West (*History of the Catholic Church in Western Canada*, Toronto: Musson 1910).

Philip Carrington offers a very general study of the history of the Anglican church in Canada (*The Anglican Church in Canada, a History* (Toronto: Collins 1963). It should be supplemented by work with a more specific focus, such as the biographical studies by T.R. Millman of the first two bishops of Quebec, *Jacob Mountain: First Lord Bishop of Quebec* (Toronto: University of Toronto 1947) and *The Life of the Right Reverend, the Honourable Charles James Stewart* (London: Huron College 1953); F.A. Peake's study of the church in British Columbia (*The Anglican Church in British Columbia*, Vancouver: Mitchell 1959); Judith Fingard's study of the church in the old colony of Nova Scotia (*The Anglican Design in Loyalist Nova Scotia*, London: SPCK 1972); T.R. Millman and A.R. Kelley's study of the church in Atlantic Canada (*Atlantic Canada to 1900: A History of the Anglican Church*, Toronto: Anglican Boot Centre 1983); and John Irwin Cooper's study of the Anglican diocese of Montreal (*The Blessed Communion: The Origins and History of the Diocese of Montreal, 1760–1960*, Montreal: Archives Committee of the Diocese of Montreal 1960).

Methodism has enjoyed the attention of many historians in the past, but their work is now showing its age. The best of the older studies is Alexander Sutherland, *Methodism in Canada: Its Work and*

Its Story (Toronto: Methodist Mission Rooms 1904). If one wishes to taste the true flavour of the rich genre of Victorian denominational studies – in itself a body of important historical material – one should read the work of the most famous and prolific historian of Canadian Methodism, the Reverend John Carroll. A good selection of his work may be found in John Webster Grant's collection *Salvation! O the Joyful Sound* (Toronto: Oxford 1967). Presbyterians receive a brief treatment in N.G. Smith, A.C. Farris, and N.K. Markell, *A Short History of the Presbyterian Church in Canada* (Toronto: Presbyterian Publications 1965). They receive a richer and more detailed analysis in John Moir, *Enduring Witness: A History of the Presbyterian Church in Canada* (Toronto: Presbyterian Church 1974), and in Laurie Stanley, *The Well-Watered Garden: The Presbyterian Church in Cape Breton, 1798–1860* (Sydney, NS: University College of Cape Breton 1983). The relationship between the Methodist and Presbyterian churches, especially in relation to church union, has received considerable attention. An older study by C.E. Silcox (*Church Union in Canada: Its Causes and Consequences*, New York: Institute of Social and Religious Research 1933) contains much useful information, but it should be read in concert with an excellent article on the intellectual and theological origins of union by Burkhard Kiesecamp ("Presbyterian and Methodist Divines: Their Case for a National Church in Canada, 1875–1900," *SR* 2 (1973): 289–302), and with Keith Clifford's recent study of the anti-unionist position, *The Resistance to Church Union in Canada, 1904–1939* (Vancouver: University of British Columbia Press 1985).

A recent collection of essays edited by Dennis L. Butcher et al., *Prairie Spirit* (Winnipeg: University of Manitoba Press 1985), offers some twenty papers on the history of the United Church in the Canadian West. It includes material on a wide range of individuals, congregations, and issues, and very useful research guides to archival holdings. The Baptists have been examined in an older study by E.R. Fitch (*The Baptists of Canada: A History of their Progress and Achievements*, Toronto: Standard Publishing 1911), as well as in two more recent regional studies: G.E. Levy, *The Baptists of the Maritime Provinces 1753–1946* (Saint John, NB: Barnes-Hopkins 1946), and S. Ivison and F. Rosser, *The Baptists in Upper and Lower Canada Before 1820* (Toronto: University of Toronto Press 1956). A more recent collection edited by Jarold Zeman, *Baptists in Canada: Search for Identity Amidst Diversity* (Burlington, Ont.: G.R. Welch 1980), addresses a wider range of topics, while Barry M. Moody, ed., *Repent and Believe: The Baptist Experience in Maritime Canada* (Hantsport, NS: Lancelot 1980) offers essays on the Atlantic regions. One should also read the biography of the famous Maritime leader, Henry Alline, written by J.M. Bumsted (*Henry Alline 1748–1784*, Toronto: University of Toronto Press 1971). For other Protestant groups see A.G. Dorland, *A History of the Society of Friends in Canada* (Toronto: Macmillan 1927); Carl R. Cronmiller, *A History of the Lutheran Church in Canada* (n.p.: Evangelical Lutheran Synod 1961); E.E. Gray, *Wilderness Christians: The Moravian Mission to the Delaware Indians* (Toronto: Macmillan 1956); Philip Hewett, *Unitarians in Canada* (Toronto: Fitzhenry and Whiteside 1978); James Penton, *Jehovah's Witnesses in Canada* (Toronto: Macmillan 1976); and Robert G. Moyles, *The Blood and Fire in Canada: A History of the Salvation Army* (Toronto: Peter Martin 1977).

To a certain extent, all religious groups in Canada have had, at least at one point in their history, a strong ethnic and cultural identification. While most major Protestant groups and the Roman Catholic church have lost this type of association, there are still a number of groups for whom religion, ethnicity, and culture are to a considerable degree coterminous. The studies of these groups are perforce studies of their respective religions. This work tends to be more social and cultural in character than the standard denominational studies. Some of the best work here includes Victor Peters, *All Things Common: The Hutterian Way of Life* (Minneapolis: University of Minnesota Press 1965); George Woodcock and Ivan Avakumovic, *The Doukhobors* (Toronto: Oxford 1968); and Frank H. Epp, *Mennonites in Canada*, two volumes (Toronto: Macmillan 1974, 1982). Two recent collections of essays, *Religion and Ethnicity* (Harold Coward and Leslie Kawamura, eds., Waterloo: Wilfrid Laurier University Press 1978) and *Visions of the New Jerusalem* (Benjamin G. Smillie, ed., Edmonton: NeWest 1983), provide both general material on this topic and studies of particular groups, especially in Western Canada.[3]

The growing interest in religion and ethnicity has also led to a number of new works on Judaism in Canada. For a general view of this recent work, one should consult two articles by Gerald Tulchinsky, "Recent Developments in Canadian Jewish Historiography" (*Canadian Ethnic Studies* 14, no. 2 (1982): 114–25) and "The Contours of Canadian Jewish History" (*Journal of Canadian Studies* 17 (1982): 46–56). General histories include Benjamin G. Sack, *History of the Jews in Canada* (Montreal: Harvest House 1965); Stuart Rosenberg's two-volume study *The Jewish Community in Canada* (Toronto: McClelland and Stewart 1970); and Michael Brown, *Jew or Juif? Jews in Canada, 1759–1914* (Philadelphia: Jewish Publication Society 1986). Simon Belkin examines Jewish immigration and settlement in *Through Narrow Gates: A Review of Jewish Immigration, Colonization and Immigrant Aid Work in Canada, 1840–1940* (Montreal: Eagle Publishing

1966), while Stephen A. Speisman examines many of the same themes in relation to one major metropolitan centre in *The Jews of Toronto: A History to 1937* (Toronto: McClelland and Stewart 1979). Two works, one by Erna Paris (*The Jews: An Account of their Experience in Canada*, Toronto: Macmillan 1980) and one edited by M. Weinfeld et al. (*The Canadian Jewish Mosaic*, Toronto: J. Wiley 1981), focus on more contemporary and cultural concerns.

RELIGION AND SOCIETY

For the presentation of monographs the two authors preferred to divide the task according to linguistic criteria, since each is more familiar with works written in his own mother tongue. William West-fall will cover works in English, and Guy Laperrière works in French. As well, each author took the approach he felt was most useful to his purposes: Westfall has sought to present the overall body of production in its essential elements, while Laperrière has restricted his discussion to works published since 1975, as he felt that the overall production in French of the last twenty-five years was much too extensive to deal with here.

Following is, first, a massive body of works that study the churches in their institutional aspects and attempt to define the reciprocal relationship between religion and society. This will be followed by the discussion of a certain number of works dealing with identity and culture, new avenues of research, and current problems.

Religion and Society – Works in English

"In view of the historical importance of religion in Canada," R.C. Stewart Crysdale remarks, "it seems strange that the basic work of conceptualization and theory should be at such an elementary level" (Crysdale and Montminy, *Religion in Canada*, p. 209). The relation-ship between religion and society has provided the focus for some of the greatest works of sociology (one thinks of Durkheim, Pareto, and Weber, as well as Marx and Parsons); in English Canada, how-ever, there is only one body of work that tries to address this re-lationship in anything like a systematic fashion. Samuel Delbert Clark rebelled against what he saw as the static concerns of American sociologists, trained his eyes on the process of social change, and placed the study of religion as a major item on the agenda of social analysis in Canada. In three important works,[4] Clark argues that the changing structure of religious organization provided a measure of the pace and character of social change. His studies were wide-ranging; he examined, for example, revivalistic movements in eighteenth-century Nova Scotia and various strains of Western Canadian radicalism. Clark undoubtedly made the study of religion an important topic in Canadian sociology. At the same time, however, his work tended to limit the range of sociological concerns by linking the study of religion to questions of the forms of religious organization and politics. Clark himself, for example, was the general editor of a series of studies on the background and development of the Social Credit movement in Alberta. Four of these studies, by C.B. Macpherson, W.L. Morton, John Irving, and W.E. Mann, are especially valuable for students of religion in Canada.[5]

The study of politics provided, in fact, one of the points at which religion entered the traditional narrative of Canadian national development. Since politics has always been one of the primary themes in Canadian studies, the religious dimensions of political issues became one of the few aspects of Canadian religion that received a reasonable degree of scholarly attention. Two books, John Moir's *Church and State in Canada West: Three Studies in the Relation of Denominationalism and Nationalism 1841–1867* (Toronto: University of Toronto Press 1959) and Alan Wilson's *The Clergy Reserves of Upper Canada: A Canadian Mortmain* (Toronto: University of Toronto Press 1968), examine the complex political issues that surrounded the changing nature of the relationship between church and state in the pre-Confederation period. The role of the Wesleyan Methodists in the politics of the same period is examined in a fine study by Goldwin French, *Parsons and Politics: The Role of the Wesleyan Methodists in Upper Canada and the Maritimes from 1780–1855* (Toronto: Ryerson 1962), while the Catholic role is treated by J.E. Rea in *Bishop Alexander Macdonell and the Politics of Upper Canada* (Toronto: Ontario Historical Society 1974). The Jesuit Estates issue provides the subject for interesting monographs by Roy C. Dalton (*The Jesuits Estates Question, 1760–1888*, Toronto: University of Toronto Press 1968) and J.R. Miller (*Equal Rights: The Jesuits' Estates Act Controversy* (Montreal: McGill-Queen's University Press 1979).

The politics of education is another sub-theme in this area. A general two-volume study is provided in C.B. Sissons, *Church and State in Canadian Education: An Historical Study* (Toronto: Ryerson 1959). John Moir's study *Church and State in Canada West* includes a substantial section on education, especially on the politics of creating a separate school system. Catholic education, separate schools, and politics are also the subject of two books by F.A. Walker (*Catholic Education and Politics in Upper Canada*, Toronto: Dent 1955 and *Catholic Education and Politics in Ontario*, Toronto: Nelson 1964), while the impact of religion and language on education and politics in the

West during the late nineteenth and the twentieth centuries is examined in works by Manoly R. Lupul (*The Roman Catholic Church and the North West School Question* (Toronto: University of Toronto Press 1974) and Paul Crunican (*Priests and Politicians: Manitoba Schools and the Election of 1896*, Toronto: University of Toronto Press 1974). The former contains a short bibliographical essay. A useful collection of essays on the topic is provided by R.C. Brown, ed., *Minorities, Schools, and Politics* (Toronto: University of Toronto Press 1969).

The relationship between religion and education is also examined in a less specifically political context in studies of the history of the educational institutions that the churches often created. Many of these studies are now quite dated and are of only marginal value. Important recent work, however, includes Charles Murray Johnston, *McMaster University*, two volumes (Toronto: University of Toronto Press 1976); Hilda Neatby and F.W. Gibson, *Queen's University*, two volumes (Montreal: McGill-Queen's University Press 1978–83); George Rawlyk and Kevin Quinn, *The Redeemed of the Lord Say So: A History of Queen's Theological College 1912–1972* (Kingston, Ont.: Queen's Theological College 1980); John S. Moir, *A History of Biblical Studies in Canada: A Sense of Proportion* (Chico, Calif.: Scholars 1982); John G. Reid, *Mount Allison University: A History to 1962* (Toronto: University of Toronto Press 1984); D.C. Masters, *Protestant Church Colleges in Canada* (Toronto: University of Toronto Press 1966); and Laurence K. Shook, *Catholic post-secondary education in English-speaking Canada* (Toronto: University of Toronto Press 1971).

Another point at which religion flows into the mainstream is in the studies of movements of political protest and social reform. Western protest has received a good deal of attention, and a number of works consider the role of religion in shaping the various movements that organized these waves of protest. In addition to the works of Morton, Irving, Mann, and MacPherson that have already been cited, one should also consult S.M. Lipset, *Agrarian Socialism: The Cooperative Commonwealth Federation in Saskatchewan: A Study in Political Sociology* (Berkeley: University of California Press 1959), and Ian Macpherson, *Each for All: A History of the Cooperative Movement in English Canada, 1900–1945* (Toronto: Macmillan 1979). A collection of essays edited by S.D. Clark, J. Paul Grayson, and Linda M. Grayson, *Prophecy and Protest: Social Movements in Twentieth Century Canada* (Toronto: Gage 1975), provides a number of useful essays on this general theme. The biographies of some of the prominent reformers also shed considerable light on the religious context of reform: Kenneth McNaught's biography of J.S. Woodsworth (*A Prophet in Politics*, Toronto: University of Toronto Press 1959) examines the leader of the CCF, while Anthony Mardinos examines the life of another radical leader, William Irvine (*William Irvine: The Life of a Prairie Radical*, Toronto: Lorimer 1979). The Progressive leader Henry Wise Wood is studied by W.K. Rolph (*Henry Wise Wood of Alberta*, Toronto: University of Toronto Press 1950).

The attempts of religious leaders to reform society have also been analyzed in a number of studies. For important background material, one should consult W.H. Elgee, *The Social Teachings of the Canadian Churches, Protestant, the Early Period, before 1850* (Toronto: Ryerson 1964). The response of the churches to immigration is studied in articles by Keith Clifford ("His Dominion: A Vision in Crisis," *SR* 2 (1973): 315–28) and Roberto Perin ("Religion, Ethnicity and Identity: Placing the Immigrants within the Church," in Westfall, ed., *Religion/Culture*, 212–29), while the prohibition movement receives a long and detailed study by Ruth Spence (*Prohibition in Canada*, Toronto: Dominion Alliance 1919), and a shorter but more analytical treatment by Gerald Hallowell (*Prohibition in Ontario*, Toronto: Ontario Historical Society 1972). An excellent article by Ernest Forbes ("Prohibition and the Social Gospel in Nova Scotia," *Acadiensis* (Autumn 1971): 11–36) treats the movement in Nova Scotia.

The social gospel itself is examined in a number of works. Stewart Crysdale's *The Industrial Struggle and Protestant Ethics in Canada* (Toronto: Ryerson 1961) places the process of economic change and the religious response to it within the context of the moral and ethical traditions of the Protestant churches. Richard Allen's fine study *The Social Passion: Religion and Social Reform in Canada, 1914–1928* (Toronto: University of Toronto Press 1971) provides the best account of the movement, while a book by G.R. Cook, *The Regenerators: Social Criticism in late Victorian English Canada* (Toronto: University of Toronto Press 1985), attempts to locate a more divergent reform impulse in the breakdown of traditional Protestant values and beliefs. The question of religion, criticism, and social reform is also examined in Michiel Horn's study of the League for Social Reconstruction (*The League for Social Reconstruction: Intellectual Origins of the Democratic Left in Canada 1930–1942*, Toronto: University of Toronto Press 1980) and Gregory Baum's examination of the Catholic dimensions of social reform (*Catholics and Canadian Socialism: Political Thought in the Thirties and Forties*, Toronto: Lorimer, 1980). Stewart Crysdale studies the social attitudes within the United Church in a more contemporary period (*The Changing Church in Canada: Beliefs and Social Attitudes of United Church People*, Toronto: United Church House 1965), while Hans Mol presents a fascinating study of the social transformation of faith in a number of recent religious groups (*Faith and*

Fragility: Religion and Identity in Canada, Burlington, Ont.: Trinity 1985).

In attempting to reform and save society, Canadians did not restrict themselves to their own national boundaries. Foreign missions also represent an important and growing field of scholarly work. Stephen Endicott's study *James G. Endicott, Rebel Out of China* (Toronto: University of Toronto Press 1980) and Munroe Scott's two-volume *McClure: A Biography* (Toronto: Canec 1977–79) present portraits of two important missionary figures, while Alvyn J. Austin's *Saving China: Canadian Missionaries in the Middle Kingdom 1888–1959* (Toronto: University of Toronto Press 1986) offers a more general treatment of the missionary enterprise. The interplay between social reform and religious thought in Quebec is analyzed in Joseph Levitt's study of Henri Bourassa (*Henri Bourassa and the Golden Calf. The Social Program of the Nationalists of Quebec 1900–1914*, Ottawa: University of Ottawa Press 1969), and from a different perspective by W.F. Ryan in a study of the role of the clergy in the economic development of Quebec (*The Clergy and the Economic Growth in Quebec, 1896–1914*, Quebec City: Les presses de l'Université Laval 1960). A more detailed and specific analysis of the role of a religious institution in the reorganization of the Quebec economy is presented in Brian Young's excellent study of the Seminary of Montreal in the nineteenth century (*In Its Corporate Identity: The Seminary of Montreal as a Business Institution, 1816–1876*, Montreal: McGill-Queen's University Press 1986).

An important counterpoint to this generally progressive and reformist interpretation of the impact of religion on social and political reform is provided by a number of works which treat the "darker side" of the role of religion in Canadian life. Here religion finds a major place in the important themes of bigotry, racism, and anti-Semitism. Howard Palmer examined the persistence of nativism, especially as a response to immigration, in *Patterns of Prejudice: A History of Nativism in Alberta* (Toronto: McClelland and Stewart 1982), while Robert Choquette studied the intense conflict between French and English in Ontario in *Language and Religion: A History of English-French Conflict in Ontario* (Ottawa: University of Ottawa Press 1975). Anti-Semitism is a major theme in three works: Lita-Rose Betcherman studies Fascist movements in the inter-war period (*The Swastika and the Maple Leaf: Fascist Movements in the Thirties*, Toronto: Fitzhenry and Whiteside 1975); Irving Abella and Harold Troper describe in an excellent book the exclusionist policies of the Canadian government toward Jewish refugees in the 1930s (*None is Too Many: Canada and the Jews of Europe*, Toronto: Lester 1982); and David J. Bercuson analyzes Canada's attitudes toward the creation of the state of Israel (*Canada and the Birth of Israel: A Study in Canadian Foreign Policy*, Toronto: University of Toronto Press 1985).

Religion and Society – Works in French

The majority of important studies, doctoral theses in particular, that have been published over the last ten years deal with the institutional church. This is doubtless due in large part to the contents of archives, which are richer and generally more accessible for this type of approach. These works have been grouped into three chronological bodies: New France, the nineteenth century, and the twentieth century, with the lion's share going to the nineteenth century.

New France. New France has lost the "monopoly" on historical studies that it held since the mid-nineteenth century, as Serge Gagnon illustrates so well in his thesis *Le Québec et ses historiens de 1840 à 1920. La Nouvelle-France de Garneau à Groulx* (Quebec City: Les presses de l'Université Laval 1978). The religious history of New France nonetheless continues to be well served, notably by Père Lucien Campeau, who continues his *Monumenta Novae Franciae*, an oft-neglected basic work that is part of the major series *Monumenta Historica Societatis Iesu*.[6] Campeau is now in the process of bringing out the *Relations* of the Jesuits and related documents containing an unprecedented wealth of erudition. The history of the Jesuits and of Monseigneur de Laval also inspired Ghislaine Boucher, who recently published a book on the church from 1608 to 1688 in which she presents missionaries Paul LeJeune, Jérôme Lalemant, and Paul Ragueneau, together with a portrait of Monseigneur de Laval, Quebec's first bishop (1659–1688) (*Le premier visage de l'Église du Canada. Profil d'une Église naissante. La Nouvelle-France, 1608–1688*, Montreal: Bellarmin 1986). Another Jesuit, Jean-Baptiste de la Brosse, was the subject of a legend which enabled ethnologist Léo-Paul Hébert to put together an impressive dossier (*Histoire ou légende? Jean-Baptiste de la Brosse*, Montreal: Bellarmin 1984). It is true that these works deal with missionary history more than with the history of the institutional church – but then, how are we to distinguish the one from the other? Lastly, there is a study by Marc-André Bédard entitled *Les protestants en Nouvelle-France* (Quebec City: Société historique de Québec 1978), which illustrates the interest of our contemporaries in religious pluralism, as do missionary studies for those studying intercultural contacts.

The Nineteenth Century. The nineteenth century has been the subject of the most extensive historical studies within the last twenty years, to such a degree that we could sketch a complete picture using doctoral theses alone. Most of the works on religious Quebec have been concerned with ultramontanism, a Catholic ideology originating in Europe which called for the supremacy of the spiritual over the temporal, the church over the state. Mgr. Lartigue, the subject of a biography by Gilles Chaussé (*Jean-Jacques Lartigue, premier évêque de Montréal*, Montreal: Fides 1980), was its initiator, Mgr. Bourget its principal herald, and Mgr. Laflèche, studied by Nive Voisine (*Louis-François Laflèche, deuxième évêque de Trois-Rivières*, Saint-Hyacinthe: Edisem 1980), its most ardent protagonist. The ultramontane ideology itself has been analyzed by Nadia F. Eid (*Le clergé et le pouvoir politique au Québec. Une analyse de l'idéologie ultramontaine au milieu du XIXᵉ siècle*, Montreal: Hurtubise 1978), while the popular side of this movement has been described with finesse in René Hardy's excellent thesis *Les zouaves. Une stratégie du clergé québécois au XIXᵉ* siècle (Montreal: Boréal Express 1980). A book of combined works in honour of Philippe Sylvain, the initiator of these studies, rounds off the body of this research (Nive Voisine and Jean Hamelin, eds., *Les ultramontains canadiens-français*, Montreal: Boréal Express 1985). Other members of the clergy have inspired interesting studies. In an incisive thesis, Gabriel Dussault brings out the messianic aspect of the colonization efforts of Curé Labelle (*Le Curé Labelle, Messianisme, utopie et colonisation au Québec, 1850–1900*, Montreal: Hurtubise HMH 1983). Several excellent works exist on the Sulpicians: Louis Rousseau has studied their preaching (*La prédication à Montréal de 1800–1830. Approche religiologique*, Montreal: Fides 1976), Marcel Lajeunesse their cultural contribution (*Les Sulpiciens et la vie culturelle à Montréal au XIXᵉ siècle*, Montreal: Fides 1982), Brian Young their financial impact (*In Its Corporate Capacity),* and Huguette Lapointe-Roy their charitable works, particularly among the Montreal poor from 1831 to 1871 (*Charité bien ordonnée. Le premier réseau de lutte contre la pauvreté au 19ᵉ siècle*, Montreal: Boréal 1987).

Here we would like to mention works on the religious communities that were so important for Catholic revival after 1840. Two remarkable theses, by Bernard Denault and Benoît Lévesque (*Eléments pour une sociologie des communautés religieuses au Québec*, Sherbrooke: Les presses de l'Université de Sherbrooke 1975) and Marguerite Jean (*Évolution des communautés religieuses de femmes au Canada de 1639 à nos jours*, Montreal: Fides 1977), provide us with a general overview. A repertory by Paul-François Sylvestre presents their actions in French Ontario (*Les communautés religieuses en Ontario français. Sur les traces de Joseph Le Caron*, Montreal: Bellarmin 1984). With reference to the Ancien Régime in Canada, Micheline D'Allaire has made an analysis of nuns' "dowries" (*dots*) during the seventeenth and eighteenth centuries (*Les dots des religieuses au Canada français, 1639–1800. Étude économique et sociale*, Montreal: Hurtubise HMH 1986). Among the many recent monographs on particular communities are Jean-Pierre Asselin's work on the Redemptorists (*Les Rédemptoristes au Canada. Implantation à Sainte-Anne-de-Beaupré, 1878–1911*, Montreal: Bellarmin 1981), and Marie-Paule Malouin's study of the Académie Marie-Rose (1876–1911) of the Sisters of the Holy Names of Jesus and Mary (*Ma soeur, à quelle école allez-vous? Deux écoles de filles à la fin du xixᵉ siècle*, Montreal: Fides 1985). This is an appropriate place to mention the works of the Groupe de recherche en histoire de l'éducation des filles (GREF), a group studying the dichotomies of the traditional educational system: boy/girl, public/private. A first synthesis, *Les Couventines. L'éducation des filles au Québec dans les congrégations religieuses enseignantes, 1840–1960*, (Montreal: Boréal 1986), by Micheline Dumont and Nadia Fahmy-Eid, has been published.

We must not create the impression that French Canada is limited to Quebec – Acadia, Ontario, and the West would never forgive us! The history of these three Francophone Catholic groups is one of constant, and continuing, struggle, in which religion and nationalism were long associated. The battle in Acadia for an Acadian clergy and a national church is described by Léon Thériault in "L'acadianisation de l'Église catholique en Acadie, 1763–1953" (in Jean Daigle, ed., *Les Acadiens des Maritimes*, Moncton: Centre d'études acadiennes 1980, 293–369). French Ontario is extensively treated in the ecclesiastic field by Robert Choquette (*Langue et religion. Histoire des conflits anglo-français en Ontario*, Ottawa: Éd. de l'Université d'Ottawa 1977, and *L'Église catholique dans l'Ontario français du dix-neuvième siècle*, Ottawa: Éd. de l'Université d'Ottawa 1984), while the West in the nineteenth century is the object of more and more interest, including Claude Champagne's thesis on Mgr. Vital Grandin (*Les débuts de la mission dans le Nord-Ouest canadien: mission et Église chez Mgr Vital Grandin, o.m.i., 1829–1902*, Ottawa: Éd. de l'Université Saint-Paul 1983), and that of Gilles Martel on *Le messianisme de Louis Riel* (Waterloo, Ont.: Wilfrid Laurier University Press, 1984).

The Twentieth Century. The body of work on the religious history of the twentieth century is not very advanced as yet, with the exception

of the Hamelin-Gagnon synthesis mentioned above. At the institutional level, however, there is solid research in two sectors that
have attracted a lot of attention within the last twenty – and even
forty – years: ideologies and the social issue. Among works on ideologies are Richard Jones' study of the journal *L'Action Catholique* from
1917 to 1939 (*L'idéologie de "L'Action Catholique" (1917–1939)*, Quebec
City: Les presses de l'Université Laval 1974) and André-J. Bélanger's
particularly enlightening work on four ideologies from 1934 to 1968
(*Ruptures et constantes. Quatre idéologies du Québec en éclatement: La
Relève, la JEC, Cité Libre, Parti Pris*, Montreal: Hurtubise HMH 1977),
each oriented toward the question of religion's place in society. As
with the study of the social gospel in English Canada, the social
question is one of the most studied subjects in French-Canadian
religious historiography. In French Canada, this is particularly the
case for Catholic syndicalism and the CTCC (1921–1960). The second
part of Jacques Rouillard's excellent thesis (*Les syndicats nationaux au
Québec de 1900 à 1930*, Quebec City: Les presses de l'Université Laval
1979) concerns Catholic unions and reviews the issue quite credit-
ably. This is not exactly the case for the book of memoirs that the
Jesuit Jacques Cousineau published before his death (*L'Église d'ici et
le social, 1940–1960. La Commission sacerdotale d'études sociales*, Montreal: Bellarmin 1982). We know that the good father was up in arms
against P.E. Trudeau over the interpretation of the asbestos strike
of 1949: here he delivers his documented version of the role of the
Sacerdotal Commission on Social Studies.

This work by Père Cousineau leads us to a phenomenon that was
inaugurated with a flourish by the appearance in book form of the
journals of Canon Groulx in 1970 and has been growing ever since:
the publication of memoirs of the clergy. There have been several
instances, and several forms: here I would like to mention those of
Père Georges-Henri Lévesque (*Souvenances 1. Entretiens avec Simon
Jutras*, Montreal: La Presse 1983) and the remarkable critical edition
of the *Journal, 1895–1911* of the young Lionel Groulx (Giselle Huot
and Réjean Bergeron, eds., Montreal: Les presses de l'Université de
Montréal 1984). In short, the institutional church is taking no chance
of going unnoticed!

NEW AVENUES OF RESEARCH

Several of the questions in this area are the same for both English
and French Canada: secularization, new religions, cultural specific-
ity, pluralism, and ethics. Each author in turn will present the facets
he felt were the most significant: William Westfall discusses those

involving identity and culture in English Canada, and Guy Laperrière looks at new approaches and the current situation in French
Canada.

Religion, Identity, and Culture:
New Approaches in English

To a considerable degree, scholars in English Canada have tended
to treat religion as a sub-theme of a larger narrative that is essentially
political and economic in character. Religion comes into prominence
when it illuminates traditional concerns such as political conflict,
economic expansion, social reform, and the development of national
institutions. More recently, however, a number of scholars have
begun to suggest that religion has played a much more formative
role in Canadian society and culture. Religion not only responds to
the world, it also shapes the character of the world itself.

The question of religion, identity, and culture has provided a
general framework for studies treating religion as a more influential
force in Canadian life. A special edition of McMaster Divinity College's *Theological Bulletin* (3 January 1968) provided the occasion for
Goldwin French (the pre-Confederation period) and John Webster
Grant (the post-Confederation period) to address the general question of the impact of religion on Canadian culture.[7] A second essay
by French, "The Evangelical Creed in Canada" (in W.L. Morton, ed.,
The Shield of Achilles; Aspects of Canada in the Victorian Age, Toronto:
McClelland and Stewart 1968, 15–35), addresses the same general
theme. A.J.B. Johnston's study *Religion in Life at Louisbourg, 1713–
1758* (Montreal: McGill-Queen's University Press 1984) attempts to
explain the crucial role that religion played in the everyday existence
of the people. An important work by Gordon Stewart and George
Rawlyk, *A People Highly Favoured of God: The Nova Scotia Yankees and
the American Revolution* (Toronto: Macmillan 1972), emphasizes the
relationship between the religious awakening led by Henry Alline
and the emerging regional identity of Nova Scotia. The same theme
is developed in a forceful manner in George Rawlyk's study of Henry
Alline and what one might call the culture of revivalism, *Ravished
by the Spirit: Religious Revivals, Baptists, and Henry Alline* (Kingston,
Ont.: McGill-Queen's University Press 1984). The issue of religion
and identity is also explored in Thomas Flanagan's remarkable study
Louis 'David' Riel: 'Prophet of the New World' (Toronto: University of
Toronto Press 1979). In two recent articles, William Westfall exam-
ines religion and culture in Upper Canada and Ontario ("Order and
Experience: Patterns of Religious Metaphor in Early Nineteenth-

Century Upper Canada," *Journal of Canadian Studies* (Spring 1985): 5–24; "The Dominion of the Lord: An Introduction to the Cultural History of Protestant Ontario," *Queen's Quarterly* (Spring 1976): 47–70), while Neil Semple explores the way religious conceptions of childhood and salvation changed in relation to new social and institutional circumstances ("'The Nurture and Admonition of the Lord': Nineteenth-Century Canadian Methodism's Response to 'Childhood,'" *Social History/Histoire sociale* 14 (May 1981): 157–76). David R. Elliott's work on William Aberhart represents an interesting attempt to treat political ideology in a distinctive religious context ("Antithetical Elements in William Aberhart's Theology and Political Ideology," *Canadian Historical Review* (March 1978): 38–58), while A.J.B. Johnston ("Popery and Progress: Anti-Catholicism in Mid-Nineteenth Century Nova Scotia," *Dalhousie Review* 64 (1984): 146–63) and J.R. Miller ("Anti-Catholic Thought in Victorian Canada," *Canadian Historical Review* 66 (1985): 474–94) study anti-Catholicism as a part of the intellectual climate of the nineteenth century.

There is also a growing body of work on the important issue of religion, gender, and identity. In an article and a new book, Marta Danylewycz examines the complex relationship between the religious life of nuns in Montreal, the structure of religious and social thought, and the development of feminism ("Changing Relationships: Nuns and Feminists in Montreal, 1890–1925," *Social History/Histoire sociale* 14 (November 1981): 413–34; and *Taking the Veil, 1840–1920: An Alternative to Marriage, Motherhood and Spinsterhood*, Toronto: McClelland and Stewart 1987). Wendy Mitchinson examines the role of two important religious and social institutions – the Young Women's Christian Association ("The YWCA and Reform in the Nineteenth Century," *Social History/Histoire sociale* 12 (November 1979): 368–85) and the Women's Christian Temperance Union ("The WCTU: 'For God, Home and Native Land': A Study in Nineteenth-Century Feminism," in Linda Kealey, ed., *A Not Unreasonable Claim: Women and Reform in Canada*, Toronto: Women's Press 1979, 151–68) – while Joy Parr treats the religious dimensions of child emigration ("'Transplanting from Dens of Iniquity': Theology and Child Emigration," in *A Not Unreasonable Claim*, 169–84) and John Thomas examines the Deaconess movement in the Methodist Church ("Servants of the Church: Canadian Methodist Deaconess Work, 1890–1926," *Canadian Historical Review* 65 (September 1984): 371–95). Veronica Strong-Boag provides an excellent overview of the life of the pioneer Canadian feminist and religious activist Nellie McClung (introduction to Nellie McClung, *In Times Like These*, Toronto: University of Toronto Press 1972), and Ruth Compton Brouwer examines the life of

Agnes Machar ("The 'Between Age' Christianity of Agnes Machar," *Canadian Historical Review* 65 (September 1984): 347–70). One should also consult the chapter on women's studies in this volume for more work that relates to this area.

The role of religion in shaping social thought is also receiving much-deserved attention. Joseph Levitt's study *Henri Bourassa and the Golden Calf* treats Bourassa's ideas in relation to the tensions between his ultramontane ideals and the industrial character of Quebec society. A similar tension between aspiration and circumstance also informs Susan Mann Trofimenkoff's *The Dream of Nation: A Social and Intellectual History of Quebec* (Toronto: Gage 1983, translated as *Visions nationales. Une histoire du Québec*, Montreal: Éditions du Tré-carré 1986). The same author also treats religion and nationalism in *L'Action Française: French Nationalism in Quebec in the 1920's* (Toronto: University of Toronto Press 1975). The work of G.R. Cook on Canadian nationalism provides interesting material on the religious dimensions of this cultural phenomenon, especially in French Canada (*Canada and the French Canadian Question*, Toronto: Macmillan 1966, and *French Canadian Nationalism: An Anthology*, Toronto: Macmillan 1967). The relationship between religion and social thought in English Canada is treated in two excellent works. A.B. McKillop, in a pioneering work, *A Disciplined Intelligence: Critical Inquiry and Canadian Thought in the Victorian Era* (Montreal: McGill-Queen's University Press 1979), traces a series of important changes in the structure of nineteenth-century religious and philosophical thought, while Carl Berger, in *Science, God, and Nature in Victorian Canada* (Toronto: University of Toronto Press 1983), examines the close associations between natural theology and the scientific study of nature. Additional perspectives on the same period are set out in interesting articles by Michael Gauvreau ("The Taming of History: Reflections on the Methodist Encounter with Biblical Criticism," *Canadian Historical Review* 65 (1984): 315–46) and Tom Sinclair-Faulkner ("Theory Divided from Practice: The Introduction of Higher Criticism into Canadian Protestant Seminaries," *SR* 10 (1981): 321–43) on biblical criticism within the Protestant churches, by Leslie Armour on the teaching of philosophy in denominational colleges ("Philosophy and Denominationalism in Ontario," *Journal of Canadian Studies* 20 (Spring 1985): 25–38), and by Brian J. Fraser on the theology of reform in Canadian Presbyterianism ("Theology and the Social Gospel among Canadian Presbyterians: A Case Study," *SR* 8 (1979): 35–46).

Religion and native culture has also provided an area for new research in the field of religious studies. This question has, in general, been approached from two different perspectives. Many have treated native cultures in relation to the missionary efforts of the Christian churches. While some of the older material that takes this approach reflects assumptions about the quality of native life and religion that do not do justice to the richness and strengths of native cultures, some of the newer work is providing more balanced and valuable insights into this important topic. In October of 1984, the *Journal of the Canadian Church Historical Society* published a special volume (26, no. 2) on "Ethnohistory." The articles in it by Douglas Leighton ("The Ethnohistory of Missions in Southwestern Ontario") and Philip Goldring ("Religion, Mission, and Native Culture") provide a good overview of the topic. *Studies in Religion* also published a special issue, in 1980 (9, no. 2), on religion and native cultures that contains six articles a   a number of reviews of the literature that have been published recently in the area.[8] The best general history of the missionary endeavour is John Webster Grant, *Moon of Wintertime: Missionaries and the Indians of Canada in Encounter since 1534* (Toronto: University of Toronto Press 1984). The second perspective focuses more directly upon the religion and culture of the native peoples themselves. This work tends to be developed primarily by anthropologists, sociologists, and geographers; it has not in large part been taken up in published form by scholars in religious studies. For material on this important aspect of religion one should consult the essays on native studies that appear in this volume. The interface between these two approaches offers another area for new work. An important article by Roger Hutchinson combines in a very stimulating manner both of these external and internal perspectives ("The Dene and Project North: Partners in Mission," *Religion/Culture: Comparative Canadian Studies*, 391–410.)

Another gateway into the question of religion and Canadian culture is provided by studies that emphasize the religious dimensions of what one might term different forms of cultural expression, or, to use a somewhat grander phrase, religion and the cultural imagination. The collection of essays by Northrop Frye, *The Bush Garden: Essays in the Canadian Imagination* (Toronto: Anansi 1971), and the same author's *The Modern Century* (Toronto: Oxford 1967) are rich and suggestive in their approach to Canadian culture and in the way they highlight the religious contexts of Canadian life. Ronald Sutherland's work, especially *Second Image: Comparative Studies in Quebec/Canadian Literature* (Toronto: New Press 1971), emphasizes the common religious patterns that inform both English Canadian and Quebec literatures. It should be read in concert with an article by Clara Thomas that sees the relationship between the two literatures in different terms ("Crusoe and the Precious Kingdom: Fables of Our Literature," *Journal of Canadian Literature* (1972): 58–64). Another pioneering study in this field is Dennis Duffy, *Gardens, Covenants, Exiles: Loyalism in the Literature of Upper Canada/Ontario* (Toronto: University of Toronto Press 1982). Three studies of Canadian writers shed considerable light on the religious dimension of their lives and work: Clara Thomas and John Lennox, *William Arthur Deacon: A Canadian Literary Life* (Toronto: University of Toronto Press 1982); Elspeth Cameron, *Hugh Maclennan: A Writer's Life* (Toronto: University of Toronto Press 1981); and David G. Pitt, *E.J. Pratt, The Truant Years, 1882–1927* (Toronto: University of Toronto Press 1984). Other important works in this area are D.J. Dooley, *Moral Vision in the Canadian Novel* (Toronto: Clarke, Irwin 1979); G.V. Fisher, *In Search of Jerusalem: Religion and Ethics in the Writings of A.M. Klein* (Montreal: McGill-Queen's University Press 1975); and a stimulating article by William James ("The Canoe Trip as Religious Quest," *SR* 10 (1980): 151–66) that treats the theme of the religious quest in the works of certain writers. In the summer of 1983, *The Journal of Canadian Studies* published a special volume on "Religion and Literature" containing a number of very interesting articles, including an overview of religion in Quebec literature by Ben-Z. Shek, a thematic study by Dennis Duffy, an essay by Barbara Helen Pell on Morley Callaghan and Hugh Hood, and a hermeneutical analysis of Henry Alline's autobiography by Jamie Scott.[9]

The work on religion and other forms of cultural expression is, unfortunately, not nearly as rich. The religious context of Canadian painting has not been explored in any systematic manner, although a number of works on individual artists allude to the religious sensibilities of their subjects. Maria Tipett's study *Emily Carr: A Biography* (Toronto: Oxford 1979) is sensitive to this dimension, but should be read in concert with an article on the same artist by Alish Farrell ("Signs of Reform: Aspects of a Protestant Iconography," *Religion/Culture: Comparative Canadian Studies*: 317–29). Architecture has also received some treatment, although even the best work here tends to tell one more about the manner of building than about the religious assumptions that the architecture expressed. Marion MacRae and Anthony Adamson's *Hallowed Walls: Church Architecture of Upper Canada* (Toronto: Clarke, Irwin 1975) is a detailed and scholarly study of church building in the pre-Confederation period; Barry Downs, in *Sacred Places: British Columbia's Early Churches* (Vancouver: Douglas and McIntyre 1980), provides an interesting and well-illustrated volume on early church-building in British Columbia that includes the religious architecture of the native peoples; Albert Tuck's study

Gothic Dreams (Toronto: Dundurn 1978) is an architectural biography of the Maritime architect William Critchlow Harris. Music, sculpture, and other art forms have received almost no attention.

New Approaches: Works in French

The most noticeable characteristic of religious studies in French Canada over the last fifteen years is the fact that they have broken out in all directions. It is therefore difficult to categorize them: the headings "history," "anthropology," "sociology," "linguistics," "catechism," "pastoral," and "theology" have become interchangeable. The boundaries have been swept away, and the subject has become interdisciplinary. Quite often, areas which in the past were studied within a perspective of conquest are today receiving renewed attention; among these are spirituality, missions, and the arts, as well as the field of practices and beliefs, which has taken on the name "popular religion." Let us take a closer look at all of this.

Following the phase of virulent secularization in the years 1968–1972, Quebec society returned to a more open view of the various forms of spirituality – and the same seems to hold true for Acadia and French Ontario, judging by the success of the charismatic movement. Apart from the movement toward Eastern spiritualities, there is a trend – small as yet, but tenacious – toward Quebec mysticism, whose principal figure is Marie de l'Incarnation (1599–1672). Several books on her have appeared, including those by Dom Guy-Marie Oury, Robert Michel, and Ghislaine Boucher.[10] The importance of the sacred in the symbolic universe of native peoples is well known, and the journal *Recherches amérindiennes au Québec* has devoted a special issue to the subject ("Le sacré," 8, no. 2, 1978). While much study is devoted to native life – including religion – from a perspective of cultural contact, the same holds true for new missionary studies, such as Jacques Langlais' *Les jésuites du Québec en Chine* (Quebec City: Les presses de l'Université Laval 1979).

But the area that saw the most development between 1971 and 1984 is popular religion. It would be impossible here to describe all of the amazing quantity of books, large and small, in the field, but a few directions can be indicated. The father and apostle of this movement was the Dominican monk Benoît Lacroix, who, after compiling a bibliography with Madeleine Grammond (*Religion populaire au Québec. Typologie des sources. Bibliographie sélective (1900–1960)*, Quebec City: IQRC 1985), collected his articles in a book entitled *La religion de mon père* (Montreal: Bellarmin 1986). The series of international and interdisciplinary conferences organized by Lacroix ended in 1982. A list of the eleven conferences, and the eight publications resulting from them, is given at the beginning of *Religion populaire, religion de clercs?* (Quebec City: IQRC 1984), the last in the series; also worth noting is *Les pèlerinages au Québec* (Pierre Boglioni and Benoît Lacroix, eds., Quebec City: Les presses de l'Université Laval 1981), in which the unity of the theme is more apparent. In their examination of the religion "of the people," Serge Gagnon and René Hardy (eds., *L'Église et le village au Québec, 1850–1930. L'enseignement des Cahiers de prônes*, Montreal: Leméac 1979); have analyzed collected sermons with their students, placing them on the grid (or gridiron) of the social framework. The teachings of the church were for the most part imparted by the "abbreviated catechism," learned by heart by generations of schoolchildren. A team led by the energetic Raymond Brodeur was set up at Laval University, and recently published its first work (Raymond Brodeur and Jean-Paul Rouleau, eds., *Une inconnue de l'histoire de la culture: la production des catéchismes en Amérique française*, Sainte-Foy, Que.: Éd. Anne Sigier 1986). Finally, Clément Légaré and André Bougaïeff have produced a semiolinguistic study of "sacred profanity" – a phenomenon peculiar to French Canada – in which they see first and foremost "a popular intensive" (*L'empire du sacre québécois. Étude sémiolinguistique d'un intensif populaire*, Quebec City: Les presses de l'Université Laval 1984).

The natural progression from popular religion is to popular arts and traditions, the study of which underwent unprecedented growth with the rise of the nationalist current from 1972 to 1980. Several works resulted, three of which are mentioned here – all of superior quality, and all completely different: a folklore study by Denise Rodrigue, *Le Cycle de Pâques au Québec et dans l'Ouest de la France* (Quebec City: Les presses de l'Université Laval 1983); another by Pierre Lessard entitled *Les petites images dévotes* on holy pictures and their traditional use in Quebec (Quebec City: Les presses de l'Université Laval 1981); and John R. Porter and Jean Trudel's excellent study of the history and reconstitution of *Le Calvaire d'Oka* (Ottawa: Galerie nationale 1974). And thus we enter into the domain of the history of religious art, which has also made huge strides since 1972, paving the way for the exhibit *Le Grand Héritage*, with its catalogue entitled *L'Église catholique et les arts au Québec* (Quebec City: Musée du Québec 1984). The catalogue mainly presents paintings, but sculpture, precious metals, ornaments, engravings, and ethnographical objects are also featured, and the whole is organized into a highly stimulating thematic plan developed by a team of specialists. Other studies have been published on the history of religious art in general, and on religious architecture in particular: Robert Lahaise's thesis *Les édifices conventuels du Vieux Montréal: aspects ethnohistoriques* (Montreal: Hurtubise HMH 1980) and Nicole Tardif-Painchaud's *Dom Bellot et l'architecture religieuse au Québec* (Quebec City: Les presses de l'Université Laval 1978) are examples, and there are many, many more. The same goes for literature, and here I will limit myself to mentioning a work by Jean Laflamme and Rémi Tourangeau, entitled *L'Église et le théâtre au Québec* (Montreal: Fides 1979), which looks at the relationship between church and theatre in Quebec, based upon the contents of episcopal pastorals.

Thus we have seen some of the new approaches to traditional religion which have renewed its credibility in religious studies and public tastes, but which no longer accounts for the current situation of religion in French Canada, which we shall turn to now.

The Situation Today (in Quebec)

Here, the corpus of human sciences is called into play, and more and more attention is being given to problems resulting from concrete situations and rooted in the social community. This has also had consequences in geographical terms. Since around 1967, French Canada no longer exists: Acadia, Quebec, French Ontario, and the Francophones of the western provinces form virtually independent entities. Thus, it must be excused that this discussion concentrates on Quebec; doubtless, there is just as much to be said on the other communities.

Diagnostics. Ever since the 1971 Dumont Report, which came out of the work of the task force on the church and the laity, diagnoses and analyses of the situation have been fashionable. One of the most recent and most substantial of these is the work of a group that had been involved with the Dumont Commission and wanted to take stock of the situation ten years later. This resulted in *Situation et avenir du catholicisme québécois* (Outremont, Que.: Leméac 1982), under the direction of Fernand Dumont and Jacques Racine. The first volume (*Milieux et témoignages*) examines different social groups: rural, working class, middle class, youth, clergy. The second volume (*Entre le temple et l'exil*) is a more extensive reflection, calling upon the major names in Christian activist thought in Quebec: Fernand Dumont, Paul Tremblay, Jacques Racine, and Jacques Grand'Maison. The slightly disenchanted title of this volume indicated what they feel is the present situation of the church: between the temple and exile. Another question that has been the subject of a multitude of commitments and many disillusions since Vatican II, relationships between the clergy and the laity, is discussed in *Relations clercs-laïcs. Analyse d'une crise* (Montreal: Fides 1985), the first in a collection of *Cahiers d'études pastorales*. All of these are general diagnoses furthering reflection upon fundamental problems.

Other studies are more sectorial. Monique Dumais has published *L'Église de Rimouski dans un contexte de développement régional (1963–1972)* (Montreal: Fides 1978). Several works centre on the recent development of religious communities, with Paul-André Turcotte doing some of the major work on the subject. Using the example of the Clercs de Saint-Viateur, he has analyzed the transformations brought about by the Quiet Revolution and its repercussions, through the use of sociological concepts of the loss of a structure of plausibility (*L'éclatement d'un monde. Les Clercs de Saint-Viateur et la révolution tranquille*, Montreal: Bellarmin 1981) and of pluralism, seen here as a process of de-institutionalization (*Les chemins de la différence. Pluralisme et aggiornamento dans l'après-concile*, Montreal: Bellarmin 1985). Still on the subject of religious communities, but using a totally different approach, Micheline D'Allaire has collected 150 interviews from within forty-five women's communities under the title *Vingt ans de crise chez les religieuses du Québec, 1960–1980* (Montreal: Éd. Bergeron 1983). In this collection, analysis has given way to description, and the prevailing voice is one of personal accounts. Those who are interested in religious communities should consult the *Donum Dei* series, which brought out its thirtieth issue in 1985, and the periodical *La vie des communautés religieuses*, published since 1942.

One of the traditional characteristics of the church is its concern for the poor. Another collective work of "diagnosis" examines the situation of pastoral work among society's underprivileged in *Dieu écrit-il dans les marges?* (Louis Racine and Lucien Ferland, eds., Montreal: Fides 1984). In this collection, authors have analyzed the worlds of labour, the family, churchgoers, the handicapped, homosexuals, prostitutes, and prisoners. This work is a most appropriate complement to the above-mentioned *Situation et avenir* ... Finally, Blandine Asselin discusses another fringe group in her book *Les Filles-Mères. Vivre à force de naître* (Montreal: Fides 1986).

Points of Controversy. With the works mentioned above we are entering into the realm of controversial issues, at the head of which we can place moral problems. The Department of Religious Sciences at the Université du Québec à Rimouski (UQAR) has made ethics its specialty, and its *Cahiers de recherche éthique*, begun in 1976 as a journal, has developed into a series that contributes fundamental reflections upon topical issues.

One of the most pressing of these issues is the question of women and their role in the church. The eighth volume of the *Cahiers* is devoted to the subject under the heading *Devenirs de femmes* (Montreal: Fides 1981). The Group for Interdisciplinary Studies on Women and Religion in Canada, led by Elisabeth J. Lacelle in Ottawa, has launched a series called *Femmes et religions* with two collections (*La femme et la religion au Canada français. Un fait socio-culturel. Perspectives et prospectives...*, Montreal: Bellarmin 1979, and *La femme, son corps, la religion. Approches pluri-disciplinaires*, Montreal: Bellarmin 1983). And theologian Jacques Grand'Maison, always to the fore on issues of the day, has published a work on feminism entitled *La révolution affective et l'homme d'ici* (Montreal: Leméac 1982).

Another sensitive issue is education. For more than fifteen years, educational denomination in Quebec has been the subject of endless and sombre debate. An ACFAS conference in 1983 attempted to define the main issues at stake, one of its most publicized episodes being the attempts to transform the Montreal school Notre-Dame-des- Neiges from a Catholic into a pluralist institution. [11] The debate is not centred at the structural level alone, but also turns on the subject of religious instruction in the school. Along with the choice between catechism and morals at the primary level, efforts were made to introduce an option of "religious culture" at the secondary level. Fernand Ouellet has given us an exhaustive study on this issue, comparing American, English-Canadian, and Quebec experiments in the area (*L'étude des religions dans les écoles. L'expérience américaine, anglaise et canadienne*, Waterloo, Ont.: Wilfrid Laurier University Press 1985). Another conference examined the question of *La religion dans la formation fondamentale au collégial* (Quebec City: Coordination provinciale des sciences de la religion 1981). Here I should mention psychological studies on religions, two of which, appropriately enough, look at religion and adolescence: one by Réginald Richard and Elisabeth Germain (*Religion de l'adolescence. Adolescence de la religion. Vers une psychologie de la religion à l'adolescence*, Quebec City: Les presses de l'Université Laval 1985), the other by Marguerite Lavoie (*Une religion de sens pour des adolescents nouveaux*, Montreal: Bellarmin 1983). In the same area, Gisèle Saint-Germain has done interesting research on the relationship between psychotherapy and spiritual orientation, based upon a three-year experiment with five nuns (*Psychothérapie et vie spirituelle. Expériences vécues*, Montreal: Fides 1979).

Pluralism and New Religious Groups. We have already spoken of pluralism: to a certain extent, pluralism is, at the secular level, the equivalent to ecumenism at the religious level. French Canadians in

Quebec, who had long been bound by their race and religion, realized that if they wanted to call themselves "Québécois" they would
have to open their circle to other ethnic groups living particularly
in Montreal, and whose religion, other than Catholic, is part of their
nationality. The existence and repression of Francophone Protes-
tantism in nineteenth-century Quebec became the subject of increasing attention.[12] On the theme of the connection between religions
and nationalism in Canada and Quebec, an issue of an international
journal on the sociology of religion, *Social Compass*, discussed the
situation of Protestants and Jews (Jacques Zylberberg et al., "Religions et nationalismes. Canada et Québec/Religions and National-
isms. Canada and Quebec," *Social Compass* 31, no. 4 (1984): 327–
438). Again on the Jewish situation, the Institut québécois de recherche sur la culture (IQRC), founded in 1979, has produced a bibliography and a collection of studies that give a major place to the
history and consciousness of the Quebec Jewish community (David
Rome et al., eds., *Les Juifs du Québec. Bibliographie rétrospective annotée*,
Quebec City: IQRC 1981; Pierre Anctil and Gary Caldwell, eds., *Juifs
et réalités juives au Québec*, Quebec City: IQRC 1984). David Rome, a
pioneer in the field, has published with Jacques Langlais a synthesis
on the history of the relationship between Jews and Francophone
Quebecers (*Juifs et Québécois français. 200 ans d'histoire commune*, Montreal: Fides 1986) which complements previous research by Victor
Teboul (*Mythe et images du Juif au Québec. Essai d'analyse critique*,
Montreal: De Lagrave 1977). Also worth mentioning in this area is
the publication, since 1977, of a semi-annual periodical, *Canadian
Jewish Historical Society Journal Société de l'histoire juive canadienne*,
which – like so many other English-Canadian periodicals – is bilingual only in name and intention. Jews are not the only minority
to have been subjected to the hostility of French-Canadian Catholics.
In the early 1950s, a celebrated battle pitted religious and civil authorities in Quebec against the preachings of the Jehovah's Witnesses – particularly during the Roncarelli Affair, a history of which
was recently published (Michel Sarra-Bournet, *L'affaire Roncarelli.
Duplessis contre les Témoins de Jéhovah*, Quebec City: IQRC 1986).

The pluralism and the upheavals which marked the period 1968–
1972 prepared the field for the appearance of new religious groups
which, even though they may concern small numbers of people,
have proliferated, and have been the subject of several academic
studies. The charismatic movement, which appeared in Quebec in
1971, has perhaps been the most widespread of these new groups
(in Acadia and French Ontario as well), and is also the one which
has been the most easily recuperated by the Catholic church.[13] Nor
to be neglected are the Catholic-oriented communes that have re-

treated into rural areas to live out a particular aspect of the Christian message. Yvonne Bergeron studied two of these in the early seventies, Les Apôtres de Jésus par Marie and Le Printemps, a descendant of L'Arche (*Fuir la société ou la transformer? Deux groupes de chrétiens parlent de l'Esprit*, Montreal: Fides 1986). Roland Chagnon continues his research into new religions, particularly scientology, in his works *La Scientologie: une nouvelle religion de la puissance* (Montreal: Hurtubise HMH 1985) and *Trois nouvelles religions de la lumière et du son* (Montreal: Éditions Paulines 1985). The ensemble of roughly three hundred "new religions" can be found in Richard Bergeron's popular book (*Le cortège des fous de Dieu. Un chrétien scrute les nouvelles religions*, Montreal: Éditions Paulines 1982), which divides them into the two main categories of sect and gnosis and attempts to give them a Christian interpretation. An important international conference on the subject, *Les mouvements religieux aujourd'hui* (1984), first examined the theoretical viewpoints on the sacred and religious movements, and then analyzed the practices of six very different religious movements, from religious orders to abstentionists, Christian feminists to Montreal Hassidim, the militant Christian left to the charismatics. Proceedings of the conference make up Volume 5 of the *Cahiers de recherches en sciences de la religion* (Jean-Paul Rouleau and Jacques Zylberberg, eds., *Les mouvements religieux aujourd'hui. Théories et pratiques*, Montreal: Bellarmin 1984).

CONCLUSION

The study of religion within the general study of Canada has, in some respects, come full circle. Exiled for too long to the margins of Canadian scholarly life, religion now shows signs of reasserting itself as a legitimate field of study. The work that has been done in the last few years provides hope that religion will be able to move beyond the denominational and institutional framework that protected the study of religion in Canada for so long, and will take its place at the heart of discussions in human and social sciences. The new avenues of research on ethnic groups, women, the family, education, economic cycles, social debates, the arts – and the list could go on – lead us to believe that religious studies, having proved itself to be an excellent point of observation, could become fully integrated into these new approaches. At the moment, much of this new work is still contained in graduate theses and articles. If it flowers into larger studies, the field of human sciences overall will be the richer for it, and another bibliographical essay will have a much richer and more varied field to explore.

NOTES

* The authors would like to express their thanks to Roberto Perin, who kindly offered his opinions on various drafts of this text, and to Roger Hutchison, Phyllis Airhart, Neil Semple, Louis Rousseau, Ruth Brouwer, and Stewart Crysdale, who all made helpful suggestions along the way. To the Secretarial Services of York University we extend our special thanks for helping to complete a difficult task in a thorough and professional manner.

1 The text of the play and a dossier on the controversy that surrounded the presentation of the play in 1978 were published: Denise Boucher, *Les fées ont soif* (Montreal: Éd. Intermède 1979).

2 The three volumes are H.H. Walsh, *The Church in the French Era* (Toronto: Ryerson 1966); John S. Moir, *The Church in the British Era* (Toronto: McGraw-Hill Ryerson 1972); and John Webster Grant, *The Church in the Canadian Era* (Toronto: McGraw-Hill Ryerson 1972).

3 For a more detailed study of ethnicity and immigration, see the relevant sections of Donald Avery and Bruno Ramirez's essay in this collection. One should also consult R. Perin, "Clio as an Ethnic: The Third Force in Canadian Historiography," *Canadian Historical Review* 64 (December 1983): 441–67.

4 *The Social Development of Canada* (Toronto: University of Toronto Press 1942); *Church and Sect in Canada* (Toronto: University of Toronto Press 1948); and *Movements of Political Protest in Canada, 1640–1840* (Toronto: University of Toronto Press 1959). See also Harry H. Hiller, "The contribution of S.D. Clark to the sociology of Canadian religion," *SR* 6 (1976–7): 415–27.

5 C.B. MacPherson, *Democracy in Alberta: Social Credit and the Party System* (Toronto: University of Toronto Press 1953); W.L. Morton, *The Progressive Party in Canada* (Toronto: University of Toronto Press 1950); John A. Irving, *The Social Credit Movement in Alberta* (Toronto: University of Toronto Press 1959); and W.E. Mann, *Sect, Cult, and Church in Alberta* (Toronto: University of Toronto Press 1955).

6 Lucien Campeau, *Monumenta Novae Franciae* (Rome/Quebec City: Monumenta Historica Societatis Iesu/Les presses de l'Université Laval). Volume 1: *La première mission d'Acadie (1602–1616)* (1967). Volume 2: *Établissement à Québec (1616–1634)* (1979). See also *La mission des jésuites chez les Hurons, 1634–1650* (Montreal: Bellarmin 1987).

7 Goldwin S. French, "The Impact of Christianity on Canadian Culture and Society before 1867," 16–18, and J.W. Grant, "The Impact of Christianity on Canadian Culture and Society, 1867 to the Present," 38–56.

8 John Webster Grant, "Missionaries and messiahs in the northwest," *SR* 9 (1980): 125–36; Aoke Hultkrantz, "The Problem of Christian influence on Northern Algonkian eschatology," *SR* 9 (1980): 161–84. There are also three articles in the following issue of the same journal: David Nock, "The failure of the CMS native church policy in Southwestern Ontario": 269–86; J.W.E Newberry, "The Quality of Native Religion": 287–98; and Antonio R. Gualtieri, "Canadian missionary perceptions of Indian and Inuit culture and religious traditions": 299–314.

9 The special issue is *Journal of Canadian Studies* 18 (Summer 1983). Among the most helpful articles are Barbara Helen Pell, "Faith and Fiction: The Novels of Callaghan and Hood": 5–17; Ben Z. Shek, "Bulwark to Battlefield: Religion in Quebec Literature": 42–57; Dennis Duffy, "Heart of Flesh: Exile and Kingdom in English Canadian Literature": 58–70; and Jamie S. Scott, "'Travels of My Soul': Henry Alline's Autobiography": 70–90.

10 Guy-Marie Oury, *Marie de l'Incarnation (1599–1672)* (Quebec City: Les presses de l'Université Laval/Abbaye Saint-Pierre de Solesmes 1973), *Physionomie spirituelle de Marie de l'Incarnation* (Sablé-sur-Sarthe: Éditions de Solesmes 1980); Robert Michel, *Vivre dans l'Esprit: Marie de l'Incarnation* (Montreal: Bellarmin 1975), translation: *Living in the Spirit with Mary of the Incarnation* (1986); Ghislaine Boucher, *Du centre à la croix: Marie de l'Incarnation (1599–1672). Symbolique spirituelle* (Montreal: Fides 1976). Boucher has also studied the case of another seventeenth-century mystic in *Dieu et Satan dans la vie de Catherine de Saint-Augustin (1632–1668)* (Montreal: Bellarmin 1979).

11 Bernard Denault et Fernand Ouellet, eds., *Confessionnalité et pluralisme dans les écoles du Québec: les principaux enjeux du débat* (Montreal: ACFAS 1983). See also Jocelyne Durand et al., *La déconfessionnalisation de l'école ou le cas de Notre-Dame-des-Neiges.* (Montreal: Libre Expression 1980).

12 See, for instance, David-Thiery Ruddel, *Le protestantisme français au Québec, 1840–1919: "images" et témoignages* (Ottawa: Musée national de l'Homme 1983).

13 This movement is well described in a book by Roland Chagnon, *Les charismatiques au Québec* (Montreal: Québec-Amérique 1979).

TEN KEY WORKS IN FRENCH

Bélanger, André-J. *Ruptures et constantes. Quatre idéologies du Québec en éclatement: La Relève, la JEC, Cité Libre, Parti Pris.* Montreal: Hurtubise HMH 1977. A specialist in political science analyzes basic ideological trends in order to come to an understanding of the social transformations which took place in Quebec between 1935 and 1965.

Denault, Bernard and Benoît Lévesque. *Éléments pour une sociologie des communautés religieuses au Québec*. Montreal: Les presses de l'Université de Montréal 1975.

Numerous facts and an interesting perspective on the general evolution of Quebec religious communities, based on a study carried out in 1969.

Dumont, Fernand and Jacques Racine, eds. *Situation et avenir du catholicisme québécois*. 2 vols. Outremont, Que.: Leméac 1982.

Two volumes focusing on the state of Catholicism: the first deals with testimonies from specific areas, the second is devoted to reflections from committed intellectuals.

Dussault, Gabriel. *Le Curé Labelle. Messianisme, utopie et colonisation au Québec, 1850–1900*. Montreal: Hurtubise HMH 1983.

A penetrating analysis of the work of the famous Curé Labelle in colonizing the Laurentians north of Montreal.

Le Grand Héritage. 2 vols. Quebec City: Musée du Québec 1984. (Vol. 1: *L'Église catholique et les arts au Québec*; Vol. 2: *L'Église catholique et la société du Québec*.)

An overview of the role played by the Catholic church in the artistic and historical development of Quebec, prepared by two teams at the time of John Paul II's visit to Canada.

Histoire du catholicisme québécois. Montreal: Boréal Express 1984.

Only volume 3 of this extensive historical overview has appeared to date: Jean Hamelin and Nicole Gagnon, *Le xxe siècle*, in two parts. This accessible synopsis closely follows the development of the institutional church in all its aspects.

Langlais, Jacques and David Rome. *Juifs et Québécois français. 200 ans d'histoire commune*. Montreal: Fides 1986.

The course of Jewish immigration in Quebec and relations between Jews and Québécois, by a Catholic and a Jew both specifically interested in intercultural relations.

Hardy, René. *Les zouaves. Une stratégie du clergé québécois au xixe siècle*. Montreal: Boréal Express 1980.

An analytical study of the five hundred Quebec *zouaves* who crossed the ocean between 1868 and 1870 to defend the Pope and the Pontifical States.

Oury, Guy-Marie. *Marie de l'Incarnation (1599–1672)*. Quebec City: Les presses de l'Université Laval 1973.

An impressive spiritual biography of Marie de l'Incarnation by a Benedictine monk from Solesmes who has devoted several works to the mystic of New France.

Voisine, Nive and Jean Hamelin, eds. *Les ultramontains canadiens-français*. Montreal: Boréal Express 1985.

A festschrift in honour of Philippe Sylvain, this book includes twelve studies on different aspects of ultramontanism, which was the most important religious ideology in French Canada in the nineteenth century.

TEN KEY WORKS IN ENGLISH

Allen, Richard. *The Social Passion: Religion and Social Reform in Canada 1914–
1928*. Toronto: University of Toronto Press 1971.
   This is the best general treatment of the social gospel movement in Canada
   in the late nineteenth and early twentieth centuries. It focuses primarily
   upon Methodist leaders, especially in the West, and treats the movement
   within a strong religious and progressive framework.

Clark, S. D. *Church and Sect in Canada*. Toronto: University of Toronto Press
1942.
   Though somewhat dated, this work nonetheless remains one of the few
   works that attempts to address the complex relationship between the
   forms of religious organization and social change in Canada.

Cook, G. R. *The Regenerators: Social Criticism in Late Victorian English Canada*.
Toronto: University of Toronto Press 1985.
   Professor Cook argues that in many cases the movements that set out to
   reform society along religious lines led in fact to the secularization of
   English-Canadian life. The book is highly entertaining and provocative.

Danylewycz, Marta. *Taking the Veil in Montreal, 1840–1920: An Alternative to
Marriage, Motherhood and Spinsterhood*. Toronto: McClelland and Stewart
1987.
   This book is a model of feminist and religious scholarship. It examines
   the religious life of nuns in the context of the social and economic structure
   of Quebec, and traces in a fascinating way the relationship between the
   experience of nuns and the rise of feminism in Quebec.

Duffy, Dennis. *Gardens, Covenants, and Exiles: Loyalism in the Literature of
Upper Canada/Ontario*. Toronto: University of Toronto Press 1982.
   A study of certain themes in Canadian literature, Dr. Duffy's text reveals
   many insights into the religious structures of the English-Canadian cultural imagination in the nineteenth and twentieth centuries.

Grant, John Webster, ed. *History of the Christian Church in Canada*. 3 vols.
Toronto: McGraw-Hill Ryerson 1966–1972.
   This three-volume work provides one of the few general overviews of the
   history of the churches in Canada. The works are primarily institutional
   in focus; the second volume by John Moir is especially strong on the pre-
   Confederation period.

— *Moon of Wintertime: Missionaries and the Indians of Canada in Encounter since
1534*. Toronto: University of Toronto Press 1984.
   This is a good study of the history of contact between missionaries and
   native peoples in Canada. As a whole it is a balanced account of a difficult
   and controversial topic.

McKillop, A.B. *A Disciplined Intelligence: Critical Inquiry and Canadian Thought
in the Victorian Era*. Montreal: McGill-Queen's University Press 1979.
   An excellent study of the character of English-Canadian social and reli-

gious thought in the nineteenth century; it traces the restructuring of ideas about God and the world in the light of the impact of Darwinian thought on Canadian academic and philosophical life.

Mol, Hans. *Faith and Fragility: Religion and Identity in Canada*. Burlington, Ont.: Trinity Press 1985.

This book presents an interesting interpretation of the role of religion in the establishment and maintenance of group identities. It has a strong theoretical framework and an interesting argument about the nature of secularization.

Westfall, William, Louis Rousseau, Fernand Harvey, and John Simpson, eds. *Religion/Culture: Comparative Canadian Studies*. Ottawa: Association for Canadian Studies 1985.

This volume provides a good collection of new essays in both English and French that address a wide range of important issues of scholarly concern in the field of religious studies. It offers a good comparative framework for recent work in the two cultures.

CHAPTER FOUR

Immigration and Ethnic Studies

DONALD AVERY AND
BRUNO RAMIREZ

INTRODUCTION

There are many dimensions to be considered when examining the
state of ethnic studies in Canada during the 1980s, not the least of
which is the expanse and diversity of the subject. Does, for example,
the term "ethnic" apply to all cultural groups in Canada, or only to
those of non-British, non-French origin? And how does one measure
the sense of ethnic identity: "... from the standpoint of the academic
observer (objective definition), or from that of the ethnic individual
(subjective definition)"?[1] Terms such as "assimilation," "Anglo-conformity," "integration," "cultural pluralism," and "multiculturalism"
defy easy explanation, and scholars use them in a variety of ways.
Ethnic studies in Canada is therefore highly fragmented, with very
little consistency in the application of analytical concepts or scholarly
methodology. Part of the reason for this confusion is the multidisciplinary character of Canadian ethnic studies, especially since the
1960s. Historians and sociologists have been the leading practitioners
of the new ethnic literature, and they have been ably assisted by
anthropologists, political scientists, and economists. Within each of
these categories, there are a wide range of sub-specialists "and not
infrequently conflicting schools of thought and methodologies."[2]
Fortunately, this trend toward particularism has been countered by
the activities of broadly based organizations, such as the Canadian
Ethnic Studies Association, and by the work of the Multicultural
Directorate, Department of the Secretary of State. Indeed, the federal
government has, since its dramatic official commitment to multiculturalism in 1971, provided both guidance and financial support
to ethnic scholars and a wide range of ethnic associations. Provincial
governments and post-secondary institutions have also contributed

to the development of ethnic studies in Canada in the 1970s and 1980s. For example, the Ontario government has generously supported the Multicultural History Society of Ontario, and the Alberta government has been instrumental in establishing the Canadian Institute of Ukrainian Studies at the University of Alberta, Edmonton.

We have used a number of approaches to provide an effective survey of ethnic studies in Canada during the 1980s. First, a historical overview of the Canadian immigration experience is provided, followed by a brief analysis of the debate over multiculturalism. The second section discusses the range of private and government ethnic programs which have emerged since 1971, and comments on their effectiveness. The final section analyzes the major conceptual and methodological approaches to Canadian ethnic studies since the nineteenth century. Most of the emphasis, however, will be placed on the past twenty-five years, the period in which ethnic studies in Canada became a dynamic and impressive scholarly activity.

A HISTORICAL OVERVIEW

Immigration and Ethnic Issues in Canada
Pre-Confederation

This section treats Canadians of French and British origin as both immigrants and ethnics. It does not, however, discuss the experience of Canada's diverse native population, largely because a separate chapter in this book has been set aside for this purpose.

The development of the French Empire in North America has been the focus of many studies, and will receive only passing mention here. Of particular importance is the fact that there were two major French settlements in what was to become Canada: Acadia and New France. Residents of both settlements faced a formidable British military threat, to which they eventually succumbed. The Treaty of Paris (1763) permanently ceded Canada to the British Empire.

This transition from one empire to another posed an immense challenge for both French Canadians and Acadians, especially since they were now forced to live under a British and Protestant political system. Yet during the next one hundred years, French Canadians were able to preserve their ethnic identity and acquire full political rights. This achievement can be attributed to many factors, including the strength of French-Canadian cultural institutions, the skills of political and clerical leaders, and the majority status of French Canadians in Lower Canada (Quebec). The fact that most English Canadians grudgingly admitted that Canada was composed of "two nations" was also of great importance. This acceptance of limited bilingualism was evident in many aspects of Canadian political life after Confederation, but most notably in the constitutional guarantees provided in section 133 of the British North America Act. But even with the Confederation "compact" it could be argued that French Canadians were, in practice, only afforded full charter-rights status in the province of Quebec. Still, the basis for a more complete extension of bilingual rights was inherent in the Canadian constitution and in the political and social dynamics of Canadian society.

British Canadians, Anglo-Canadians, Anglo-Celts, WASP – all these terms have been used in recent years to describe Canadians whose origins can be traced to Great Britain. Yet, just as it is important to appreciate differences between Acadians and Québécois, so too it must be recognized that there were major distinctions between English, Scottish, Irish, and Welsh immigrants who came to Canada in the eighteenth, nineteenth, and twentieth centuries. Nor were these groups necessarily unified. For example, religious differences often divided Irish immigrants into rival Catholic and Protestant factions. Even the Loyalists, those famous "first Anglo-Canadians" and "un-Americans," were a varied group. For example, among the Loyalists who came to Upper Canada (Ontario) were English-speaking gentlemen from Boston and back-country farmers from Pennsylvania. Some Loyalists were German-speaking rather than Anglophones; others, such as those of the Six Nations, were red rather than white.

The large-scale movement from Great Britain to the colonies of British North America between 1800 and 1867 reinforced the Anglo-Protestant character of most of the British North American colonies. Lower Canada, where French Catholics represented approximately 70% of the population in this period, was, of course, the major exception. The Catholic character of Quebec was reinforced by the arrival of thousands of Irish Catholics, most of whom gravitated toward the rapidly expanding city of Montreal. Their integration into this new environment was not, however, always harmonious. Throughout the nineteenth century Irish immigrants often bitterly competed with French Canadians for jobs, for neighbourhoods, and even for control of Catholic parishes in the city. The Irish were also an important element in the unskilled-labour forces of Upper Canada and New Brunswick, especially in the lumber camps and as canal and railway navies. Competition between various groups of British immigrants was also evident in Newfoundland, Prince Edward Island, and Nova Scotia, but at the same time there was a growing sense of regional identity which tended to blur the older loyalties.

For many, being a Nova Scotian or a New-foundlander was becoming more important than being Scottish or Irish.

By the time of Confederation, the largest colony was Upper Canada (Ontario), followed closely by Lower Canada (Quebec). Each had a population of over one million. The ethnic character of the two provinces was, however, quite different, with Quebec being overwhelmingly French and Catholic, while Ontario was predominantly British and Protestant. The Atlantic colonies of Nova Scotia, Prince Edward Island, and Newfoundland (the last of which did not join Canada until 1949) generally followed the Ontario model. In contrast, New Brunswick, with its substantial and increasingly assertive Acadian population, was divided into two distinct linguistic groups. By the 1970s it would have the distinction of being the only officially bilingual province.

The issue of French-language rights and Catholic schools was a major element of conflict within the new nation of Canada. Although it first surfaced in New Brunswick in 1872, in many ways the most bitter educational confrontations occurred in the newly created province of Manitoba (1870) and in the North West Territories (Saskatchewan and Alberta, 1905). The federal government, in its policies aimed at the Métis (persons of mixed Indian and French origin) and the Plains Indians, had to respond to another set of ethnocultural values and institutions. That the federal government, and white society in general, failed to appreciate the unique cultural characteristics of these original inhabitants of the region remains one of Canada's great historical tragedies. Nor did native people in British Columbia fare any better from provincial authorities; on the contrary, they often had great difficulty protecting their land rights and safeguarding their cultural institutions. The westernmost province also became a battleground involving another group of non-whites – Chinese immigrants.

Canada at the time of Confederation was overwhelming British in ethnic origin. Anglo-Canadians also dominated the economic and political life of the country. That is not to say, however, that French Canadians in Quebec did not exert a powerful influence on federal politics. The long domination of the Conservative Party of John A. Macdonald (1867–73; 1878–96) and of the Liberal party of Wilfrid Laurier (1896–1911) bears witness to the importance of the French-Canadian bloc vote. The question of whether French Canadians obtained the appropriate social rewards from being a part of the ruling party is an ongoing historical debate. In immigration matters, at least, the answer is No, they did not. Both the goals and recruitment strategies were determined by English Canadians – sometimes, in the face of opposition from Quebec.

Immigration Strategies and Ethnic Co-existence 1867–1940

Immigration recruitment in the three decades after Confederation was not very successful. A large majority of the emigrants from western Europe and Great Britain felt that economic and social opportunities were far superior in the United States. In fact, many nineteenth-century Canadians were similarly attracted by "the American way of life," and by 1900 over a million former Canadians had located in the United States.

The election of the Liberal government of Wilfrid Laurier in 1896 was followed by a marked expansion of immigration into Canada. The change in administration had coincided with a period of worldwide prosperity which, in a Canadian context, focused attention on the development of the West. To make this dream a reality, strong and willing workers were needed to cultivate the vast expanse of virgin prairie, to build the transcontinental railroads, and to supply the manpower for a burgeoning industrial system. Thus, the new government turned with greater enthusiasm than did its predecessors to attracting new immigrants not only from the traditional sources (Great Britain, western Europe, and the United States), but also from central and eastern Europe. One aspect of the immigration debate revolved around the importance of racial and cultural characteristics as criteria for entry into Canada. Although many entrepreneurs pressed for the large-scale importation of non-white immigrants who would function as an industrial proletariat, Canadian public opinion was generally hostile to the entry of ethnic groups that were believed to be non-assimilable. The undesirable qualities of the non-white races, it was argued, sprang from genetic and racial determinants which would not be altered by contact with Canadian society.

Few restrictive measures were imposed against Caucasian immigrants. Despite some unsatisfactory behavioural traits ascribed to certain ethnic and national groups from Europe, Anglo-Canadian immigration "boosters" claimed that these traits were primarily based on their past cultural and environmental background. Time and Anglo-Canadian institutions, it was held, would ultimately erase these differences and facilitate the absorption of all white immigrants into the Anglo-Canadian community. Most Canadians accepted these assurances, but there were certain elements in the country that reacted negatively toward these European newcomers. Organized labour, for instance, charged that immigration recruitment produced a continuous supply of cheap labour which permitted the business community to resist trade-union demands for higher wages, better working conditions, and union recognition. Many French Canadians argued that instead of recruiting European immigrants, the Dominion government should assist Quebec farmers to relocate in the rural areas of western Canada. Concern was also expressed that the influx of these European immigrants would alter the bicultural character of the nation, especially in the West. But, despite this opposition, Canada's immigration policy remained expansionist until the First World War.

The rapid growth in Canada's population which occurred between 1896 and 1930, and the accompanying ethnic diversification, had critical implications for the future of the country. While the settled regions of eastern Canada retained their English-French cultural dualism, the developing regions to the north and west of the Great Lakes assumed many of the characteristics of a pluralistic society. The emergence of ethnic communities played a useful role in helping their members to adjust from one linguistic environment to another, and sometimes from a rural way of living to an urban one. However, in some cases, the ethnic community acted as a brake on the individual achievement and social mobility of its members. Economic and cultural discrimination from both the Anglophone and Francophone host societies also created difficulties for many immigrants, a trend which was exacerbated by the severe problems associated with the Great Depression.

Prior to 1930, Anglo-Canadians had often demonstrated concern over the slow rate of Canadianization among certain immigrant groups. During the First World War, patriotic fervour had brought about the abolition of bilingual schools in western Canada and a temporary redefinition of the citizenship rights of European newcomers on the basis of wartime service. This suspicion of divided loyalties once again surfaced in the late 1920s, when the Ku Klux Klan of Kanada, a weird hybrid of American and indigenous bigotry, enjoyed some success in Saskatchewan with its "anti-foreigner" campaign. Not surprisingly, the advent of the Great Depression intensified the fear of aliens even more, as the spectre of unemployment and social demoralization seemed to threaten the fundamentals of Canadian society.

Xenophobia became particularly pronounced in the late 1930s, when thousands of German and Austrian Jews fled the Nazi terror and sought sanctuary in the Northern Dominion. Despite anguished representation from a wide variety of Canadian humanitarian organizations and the favourable response of other "traditional" immigration countries, most notably the United States and Australia, the Canadian immigration gates remained virtually closed to these tragic refugees.

Canadian Immigration Policies Since 1945

Fortunately, the post-war years witnessed a dramatic change in Canada's refugee policy. In keeping with their new commitments to the United Nations and to human rights, Canadians welcomed over 150,000 European refugees and displaced persons between 1946 and 1952 – a substantially higher ratio of acceptance than the United States. There was, however, a dimension of economic self-interest to this generous response. Displaced persons were expected to perform traditional immigrant types of work in agriculture and in the labour-intensive extractive industries. For many of the "DPS," as they came to be called, adjustment to the Canadian environment was very difficult, especially for professionals and skilled workers. Particularly frustrating was the attitude of Canadians who underestimated these immigrants' abilities because of their unfamiliarity with the English language, and of the Canadian professional associations, which were reluctant to certify European-trained doctors, dentists, lawyers, and teachers.

The continued expansion of the Canadian economy, the seemingly insatiable demand for unskilled and skilled labour, and the heady optimism that Canada was an evolving major world power encouraged an expansionist immigration policy in the 1950s and 1960s. Thousands of Dutch, German, Italian, Greek, and Portuguese immigrants came to this country with the expectation of a better life; the low level of re-emigration suggests that most realized their goals. But now it was not the prairies that attracted most immigrants. Instead, over half of the newcomers gravitated toward the major centres of Ontario, most notably Toronto, which became, by 1970, the most culturally diverse city in the country. Significantly, most Canadians welcomed the increasingly pluralistic quality of Canadian society, and most immigrants effectively adjusted to their new environment. A wide variety of ethnic organizations (churches, newspapers, voluntary associations) have assisted in this social transition, but perhaps the most important integrationist catalyst has been the Canadian educational system, that essential bridge between Anglo-Canadian and immigrant communities.

Three federal agencies have been responsible for immigration policy since World War II: the Department of Citizenship and Immigration (1950–65), the Department of Manpower and Immigration (1966–77), and the Canada Employment and Immigration Commission (est. 1977). Although most provinces have continued to accept Ottawa's primacy in immigration matters, the Quebec government, during the Quiet Revolution of the 1960s, established its own service in order to recruit as many French-speaking immigrants as possible and to ensure that immigrants who settle in Quebec form part of the Francophone community. Immigration regulations provide for the entry of two categories of immigrants: close relatives and independent applicants determined by skill, and refugees.

Since 1967, when Canada followed the lead of the United States in removing discriminatory sections from the Immigration Act and its regulations, the selection of applicants for admission has been largely conducted on the basis of occupational training, with professional and skilled immigrants theoretically being granted entry regardless of their ethnic background. Although these principles were enshrined in the Immigration Act of 1978, there was still criticism that Canadian immigration procedures were arbitrary and discriminatory when applied to immigrants from Third World countries. As a result, during the 1980s the Immigration Bureau of the Department of External Affairs has become very much involved in those immigration programs which affect Canada's foreign policy. It is this branch of government that helps to monitor the country's international commitment to allocate at least ten per cent of its annual immigration quota for refugees. Indeed, since the 1950s Canada has accepted thousands of refugees from all parts of the world: Hungarians in 1956, Czechs in 1968, Ugandans in 1972, and, more recently, Indo-Chinese "boat people." Political refugees from Latin American dictatorships, however, have not always been as fortunate!

As the nation approaches the 1990s, the old debate over immigration policy and the ethnic character of Canadian society continues. Should Canada greatly expand its annual intake beyond the 1988 quota of 135,000? How many should come from Third World countries? To what extent do Canadians wish to extend the pluralistic character of their society? Are racism and ethnic intolerance spent forces in this country, or are they recurring phenomena which surface in periods of large-scale immigration? Given the complexity of these questions, it is little wonder that politically ambitious ministers of immigration often seek a quick exit from that portfolio!

ANGLO-CONFORMITY AND MULTICULTURALISM, 1960–1988

In most regions of Canada, the experience of successive immigrant groups has been one of assimilation, or "Anglo-conformity." While there are many definitions of this phenomenon, perhaps the most useful is that of Alan Anderson: "Assimilation refers to the dominant

group's attempts to absorb a minority group on its own terms without regard to the minority's desire. It is, then, a loss of a minority's
identity through merging with the dominant community."[3] Quite
clearly, Quebec, or more specifically Montreal, provides an exception
to this model because immigrant groups have had the option of
merging into two host societies – one English, one French.

The prevailing attitude among Anglo-Canadians until the 1960s
was that both "old" and "new" immigrant groups would eventually
be assimilated. Among Canada's ethnic groups there was a mixed
reaction to Anglo-conformist pressure. For some, most notably Germans, Dutch, and those tracing their origins to the Scandinavian
countries, assimilation was not perceived as a major problem, and,
in general, they were prepared to express their sense of ethnic identity in ways that were compatible with goals of Anglo-Canadian
society. For others, such as the Chinese, Italians, Greeks, Portuguese, Ukrainians, and Poles, there was greater cultural vitality,
institutional completeness, and ethnic enclosure. Visible minorities
such as Chinese, Japanese, and blacks were in a somewhat separate
category in that they still encountered residual prejudice and discrimination. Nevertheless, their status was much improved as protection of human rights in Canada became more the rule than the
exception. By the 1970s, therefore, most non-English, non-French
Canadians were in a position to share in the benefits associated with
the multicultural policies of the federal government.

In many ways, this form of multiculturalism must be considered
in the context of the intense debate between English Canadians and
French Canadians during the 1960s. The Royal Commission on Bilingualism became the focus of much scholarly discourse, and the
publication of its final report in 1969 had a decided impact on the
nation. But for the approximately twenty-five per cent of the population who were non-British, non-French, the discussion about
charter-group rights and official languages did not relate to their
individual and collective aspirations. This sense of cultural alienation
was especially pronounced in western Canada and in the large urban
centres of central Canada. It also found expression in the minority
report in *Book Four of the Royal Commission, the Cultural Contributions
of Other Ethnic Groups* (Ottawa 1969):

The presence in Canada of many people whose language and culture are
distinctive by reason of their birth or ancestry represents an inestimable
enrichment that Canadians cannot afford to lose. The dominant cultures
can only profit from the influence of these other cultures. Linguistic variety
is unquestionably an advantage, and its beneficial effects on the country

are priceless. We have constantly declared our desire to see all Canadians associating in a climate of equality, whether they belong to the Francophone or Anglophone society. Members of "other ethnic groups," which we prefer to call cultural groups, must enjoy these same advantages ... Finally, the presence of the other cultural groups in Canada is something for which all Canadians should be thankful. Their members must always enjoy the right – a basic one – to safeguard their languages and cultures. (Book 4, p. 14)

These arguments became the rallying cry of many ethnic organizations across the country. The federal government listened, and then responded. In October of 1971, Prime Minister Pierre Elliott Trudeau announced in the House of Commons his government's commitment to multiculturalism within a bilingual framework:

First, resources permitting, the government will seek to assist all Canadian cultural groups that have demonstrated a desire and effort to continue to develop a capacity to grow and contribute to Canada, and a clear need for assistance, the small and weak groups no less than the strong and highly organized.

Second, the government will assist members of all cultural barriers to full participation in Canadian society ...

Fourth, the government will continue to assist immigrants to acquire at least one of Canada's official languages in order to become full participants in Canadian society. (House of Commons, Debates 1971)

In short order, a minister of state responsible for multiculturalism was established within the Department of the Secretary of State. The present Multicultural Directorate was created in 1976. A parallel development was the formation of the Canadian Consultative Council on Multiculturalism, an organization composed of more than one hundred representatives of various ethnic groups to advise the Minister. Since the 1970s, the Multicultural Directorate has been involved with a variety of Canadian ethnocultural organizations. Financial support has been forthcoming for festivals, conferences, and a wide range of publications. Of great value has been the assistance that has been extended to the Canadian Ethnic Studies Association (CESA), founded in 1971 as a multidisciplinary organization committed to ethnic studies in Canada.[4] Other federal agencies have also encouraged the dissemination of quality research, most notably the Canadian Centre for Folk Culture Studies, the National Museum of Man, and the Department of Employment and Immigration.[5]

By 1978, the provinces of Ontario, Manitoba, Saskatchewan, Alberta, and British Columbia had also proclaimed policies of multiculturalism. The extent of these programs varied, but they usually involved the appointment of advisory committees on multiculturalism, financial support for conferences and folk festivals, and long-term assistance to a wide range of ethnocultural organizations and academic projects. In many ways, it was in the realm of education that the extent of government commitment to multiculturalism was most clearly revealed.

Ontario, now one of the most ethnically diverse of provinces, has demonstrated considerable interest in supporting multiculturalism. For example, the Department of Citizenship and Culture has undertaken a variety of tasks to encourage ethnic studies, including awarding research grants to various ethnic groups and ethnocultural communities in order "to begin developing an information base about the ethnocultural composition and the character of the province." Other research projects have been directed toward the educational needs of recent immigrant children and the development of multicultural materials for use in the schools of the province; the Ontario Institute for Studies in Education (OISE) has provided valuable assistance in these activities. In 1973, the Ministry of Education, as part of its multicultural policy, introduced the Heritage Language Program to maintain and develop the diversity of languages in Ontario. Under this program the Ministry provides school boards with the necessary funds to provide Heritage Language classes in the elementary schools. The special "English as a Second Language Program" is an important service offered to recent adult immigrants; it is jointly funded and operated by the Ministry of Citizenship and Culture's Newcomer Service Branch and the federal Department of the Secretary of State. The creation in 1979 of the Cabinet Committee on Race Relations is further evidence of the commitment of the Ontario government to multiculturalism.

Since 1971, various government departments and agencies have provided assistance to private institutions involved in ethnic studies.[6] Of particular note was the establishment in 1976 of the Multicultural History Society of Ontario, which has sponsored scholarly research about ethnic and immigration history through its many conferences; its publications, including *Polyphony*, with its various thematic issues; and a series of monographs on specific aspects of ethnicity in Ontario.[7]

Private Ontario organizations involved in ethnic studies include the Urban Alliance on Race Relations, the Polish Canadian Research Institute, the Association for the Advancement of Baltic Studies, The Ukrainian Professional and Business Club, The Celtic Arts Association, and the Windsor Immigrant Women's Centre. Ontario universities have also demonstrated a keen interest in various aspects of multicultural studies; two of the more active institutes and programs are located in metropolitan Toronto. Much valuable research has been conducted by the Ethnic Research Program at the Institute For Behavioural Research, York University, and the Ethnic and Immigration Studies Programme at the University of Toronto.[8] The Franco-Ontario archives and the Centre de Recherche en Civilisation Canadienne Française at the University of Ottawa have done much to advance the study of Ontario's minority charter group.[9] Ethnic studies constitutes an important part of the social science and humanities courses offered in other Ontario universities and community colleges.[10]

Western Canada, with its diverse ethnic population, has witnessed considerable support for ethnic studies in the past twenty-five years. In Manitoba, the provincial government has provided funds directly to a variety of ethnic organizations and given extensive support to the multicultural centre in Winnipeg.[11] The Mennonite Heritage Centre (Winnipeg), founded in 1973 for the study of Mennonite history and culture, has received both government and private assistance.[12] The Centre has, in recent years, been active in encouraging a number of publications. The province's large and active Ukrainian community has been well served by the Ukrainian Archives in Winnipeg. Established in the late 1970s, it has collected a wide range of materials relating to the Old World experience, Ukrainian settlement in the West, and the role that Ukrainian Canadians have assumed in Canadian society.[13]

Similar trends are evident in Saskatchewan. Multicultural museums are maintained in both Saskatoon and Regina. At the University of Regina, the Ethnic Research Section of the Canadian Plains Research Centre has published a number of useful monographs. The provincial government has also provided other services which have facilitated the awareness of multiculturalism in the province.

The other two western provinces have also provided various forms of support for ethnic studies. This is particularly the case in Alberta, where government financial assistance has been generous. For example, between 1976 and 1983 the Alberta Heritage Fund funnelled millions of dollars into a wide range of scholarly and popular ethnic programs. Of particular importance was the creation of the Canadian Institute for Ukrainian Studies at the University of Alberta.[14] British Columbia's immigration and ethnic experience has been quite different from that of the prairies. This uniqueness is expressed in the types of ethnic-studies programs that have developed in the province.[15]

The development of ethnic-studies programs in Atlantic Canada has differed considerably from that in the rest of Canada. First, there are not that many programs or organizations committed to the study of non-English, non-French Canadian ethnic groups. This is, however, gradually changing. The 1985 creation of the Society for the Study of Ethnicity in Nova Scotia, whose purpose is to support the study of ethnicity in Nova Scotia and to encourage scholarly research on ethnicity, is a most encouraging trend. The second difference is the important emphasis on the cultural history of Canada's two charter groups. There are a number of centres in the region committed to the study of Scottish, Irish, English and Welsh studies.[16] In New Brunswick, Acadian history and culture are a major commitment at the University of Moncton.[17]

QUEBEC AND MULTICULTURALISM

Historical Trends

Before Confederation, immigrants coming to Quebec had originated almost exclusively in the British Isles. By the 1860s, they made up about one-fourth of the province's total population. Their presence in the province's economic and institutional space contributed greatly to the particular bicultural character of Quebec society, while at the same time constituting a source of major political and cultural tensions.

This ethnocultural picture would become significantly altered as a result of the new wave of immigration which began in the late nineteenth century and persisted through the 1920s. Unlike some other provinces of Canada, where a sizeable portion of newcomers settled in rural areas and took up farming, in Quebec the new immigrants were attracted almost entirely to the Montreal metropolitan region. The new immigration wave served to satisfy the manpower needs of two rapidly expanding labour markets. The first one was essentially seasonal in character and closely followed the evolution of the industrial geography at both a regional and a national level, feeding on the phenomena of target migration and sojourning; the other was tributary to the development of the manufacturing industry and to the expansion of an urban economy in the metropolitan region.

There are no separate statistics of yearly immigrant entries to Quebec for this period, making it impossible to have accurate estimates of the actual volume of immigrant populations which, whether temporarily or not, occupied the Quebec space. A partial quantitative view can be obtained from the decennial census statistics, which specified the ethnic origin of the enumerated populations. Thus, we know that the ethnic population whose origins were other than French or British grew from about 26,000, in 1901, to about 158,000, in 1931. In this latter census year, more than four-fifths of that population was concentrated within the Montreal region, with Jews and Italians constituting the great majority. This means that the pluralistic character that Quebec society began to acquire from the turn of the century onward was essentially a Montreal reality, and contributed to sharpening the distinction between the metropolitan region and the rest of the province.

The insertion of this new immigrant population into Quebec urban society did not come about without social tensions and cultural conflict. This was partly due to the fact that in the Montreal region, much more, for instance, than in the Toronto region, the new immigrant population came into close contact with the native (mostly Francophone) working class, thus often competing in the same labour and housing markets. The ensuing conflict, coupled with the hostility that some sectors of the clergy showed toward non-Catholic immigrants (such as orthodox Jews) considerably favoured the emergence of a nativist sentiment. Moreover, some sectors of the French-Canadian elite tended to view the newcomers with an unfavourable eye because their arrival coincided with a major exodus of rural Quebecers to the United States. Many of them saw these population movements in and out of the province as deliberate attempts by English-Canadian elites to change the composition of the population and weaken the Francophone presence within both Quebec and Confederation.

In spite of difficulties such as these, by the 1930s the urban landscape of Montreal reflected an unmistakable pluri-ethnic character. Immigrants and their children had solidly established themselves in a variety of neighbourhoods, creating a whole range of ethnic institutions and contributing their skills and commercial know-how to the expansion of the urban economy.

The multi-ethnic character of the Montreal metropolitan region became further intensified by the wave of post-World War II immigration. Like the previous wave, this one was largely urban-directed, drawing its earliest and largest contingents from southern and eastern Europe. Changes in Canadian immigration policy effected in the 1960s, however, drew increasing proportions of immigrants from Third World countries, particularly Francophone ones.

By 1971, the population of ethnic origin other than French or

British made up twenty-four per cent of the population of the Montreal metropolitan region. Some long-established ethnocultural communities, such as the Italians and the Jews, had already experienced a degree of institutional completeness prior to World War II. Other, more recent groups, such as the Greeks and the Portuguese, reached that stage very rapidly, establishing themselves firmly within the inner-city space and exhibiting an equally significant institutional and cultural vitality.

The social climate accompanying this vast process of immigration and settlement presented characteristics some of which were not unlike those produced by the previous wave of immigration. The growing presence, for instance, of blacks and Asians tested the racial attitudes of Francophone society. Moreover, the immigrants' diversified presence within the labour market often translated itself into competitive dynamics with the native working-class population. The difficulties that some immigrants' children experienced in acceding into Catholic public schools or, later, into the English education system produced some of the most explosive situations in the province's recent past.

As we shall see below, the coming to power of the "indépendantiste" Francophone elite has created a new political and cultural context, marked by unprecedented efforts to recognize the place and the contribution of ethnic minorities and to lay down the basis for a pluralistic Quebec society.

Multicultural Programs

In Quebec, multicultural concerns and policies have been highly conditioned by the particular cultural and political atmosphere pervading the province. The intensification of a nationalist sentiment among French Canadians has contributed to a redefinition of the ethnic issue, casting it into a framework of social and political polarization. On the whole, scholars were more interested in studying the ethnic traits of French Canada as a "founding nation" ("la québécitude") than in trying to understand the place of the various ethnocultural communities in the development of Quebec society. As we shall see, this was one of the leading factors behind the late development of ethnic studies within French-Canadian scholarship; it was also one of the reasons for the suspicion with which French-Canadian intellectuals tended to view federally promoted multicultural programs and policies in the province.

The lack of intellectual legitimacy that multiculturalism suffered among growing sectors of the Francophone elite did not prevent federal authorities from implementing multicultural programs within the province's ethnocultural communities. Associational life and activities among such communities could thus develop much as they did in other provinces. On several occasions, it was through these associations that federal funds were channelled in order to undertake local ethnic research – often with dubious results. By the mid-1970s, however, there were unmistakable signs among French-Canadian scholars and intellectuals of a growing awareness of ethnic phenomena within Quebec society flowing from the immigration process. In part, this awareness had been provoked by the much-publicized tensions between French Canadians and some ethnic minorities over the issue of language rights and educational policies. Subsequently, it was also due to the "Indépendantiste" government taking the initiative in the field of ethnic relations.

The existence in Quebec of a Ministry of Immigration with some jurisdiction in the selection of immigrants destined for that province has resulted in a growing body of statistical data that were essential for the study of ethnic relations. Similarly, research on post-war demographic and linguistic trends in the province found evidence that the majority position of the Francophone population was being seriously weakened by the anglicization of immigrants settling in Quebec. Developments such as these were very instrumental in producing a change in attitude with regard to the province's multi-ethnic reality, and the most tangible signs of this change emerged in the new policy of cultural development launched by the Parti Québécois soon after its accession to power in 1976. Critical of both the assimilationist perspective and multiculturalism, the new policy was based on the principle that the ethnocultural diversity existing within the province was a crucial enriching element for the future development of Quebec society. Cultural pluralism would thus result from all existing ethnocultures "converging" with the majority Francophone culture – a process that had to be promoted and safeguarded by positive government action.

In practice, however, this new outlook on inter-ethnic relations was hardly distinguishable from the multiculturalist approach. Through its expanded Ministry of Immigration (which became the Ministry of Cultural Communities and Immigration), the provincial government undertook a number of programs designed to promote the associational life of ethnocultural groups and render their presence in public life more visible. By the early 1980s, the attentive observer could see two varieties of multiculturalism at work in the province, both competing for the political allegiance of ethnocultural groups: one linked to the notion of a "Canadian mosaic," the other expressing the vision of a pluralistic, but Francophone, Quebec.

One important result of these policy developments has been to make ethnicity and ethnic relations a central issue in public life, and thus to promote a new sensibility concerning the place of ethnic minorities in Quebec society. Increasingly, the "ethnic issue" has found its place on the agenda of Francophone intellectuals and researchers. The creation in 1979 of the Institut québécois de recherche sur la culture is the best illustration of the convergence of political and academic concerns on this question. From the outset, the Institut's activities have been based on a pluralist conception of culture, and thus considerable effort has been directed toward the study of ethnocultural history and relations within the Quebec context. In its first five years of activities, the Institut was responsible for a sizable body of literature on ethnic relations, of both a monographic and a bibliographic character, thus playing a vanguard role in the promotion of a multi-ethnic vision of Quebec society.[18]

An equally important part in the development of a new sensibility on the ethnic issue was played by some of the province's leading Francophone cultural magazines. Editors and writers have shown an increasing willingness to cover social and cultural events with ethnic content, in some cases devoting entire issues of their magazines to this question.

This scenario, however, would not be complete without mentioning that this new outlook on inter-ethnic relations has also been a function of cultural phenomena occurring within many ethnocultural communities in Quebec. Throughout the 1970s and the 1980s a number of New-Quebecers have made important inroads in public life, in the arts, and in the media – enough to lay the basis for a new cosmopolitanism which, to the eye of the most optimistic observer, could evolve independently from party strategies and political interference.

A SURVEY OF MAJOR TRENDS IN THE WRITING OF ETHNIC STUDIES IN CANADA

Since Confederation, the writing of ethnic history in Canada has gone through a number of stages. The first of these would be the British and French ethnocentric and patriotic works of the nineteenth century. Most of these emphasized the hardships associated with settlement, the value of their respective institutions, and the glorification of certain heroes. There were, however, major differences of emphasis between French-Canadian and English-Canadian historical works. For Francophone writers, the glories of New France and the trauma of the Conquest were the dominant themes. In more contemporary literature, these studies emphasized the difficult struggle to protect the French-Canadian Catholic culture and the important role that Quebec assumed in this ongoing crusade.[19] In contrast, historical and fictional books by Anglophones saw the Conquest and the arrival of the Loyalists as two of the most important events in Canada's development. Much emphasis was placed on the marvellous way in which Canada was evolving constitutionally, politically, and economically within the framework of the British Empire. Confederation and the settlement of the West were other themes that attracted considerable attention.[20] However, a certain degree of ethnic bias emerged in a number of these nineteenth-century Anglo-Canadian studies, directed toward native peoples, French Canadians, and Irish-Catholic immigrants.[21] The latter group, in particular, was portrayed as a turbulent ethnic proletariat which was a threat to the economic and social stability of British North America. In later years, other ethnic groups that began their Canadian odyssey from the bottom rungs of Canadian society would be ascribed an even more negative stereotype.[22]

With the arrival of thousands of immigrants from western Europe, English-Canadian writers and scholars began to change their focus somewhat. In general, these authors approached western European immigrants sympathetically, although there was still the assumption that German, Dutch, and Scandinavian immigrants did not quite measure up to the cultural qualities of British immigrants or Anglo-Canadian society. At the same time, a body of literature began to emerge from these ethnic groups themselves, which discussed their respective North American experiences. Unfortunately, most of these works were published in the United States and lacked the necessary Canadian context and perspective.[23]

In the 1900s, the "stalwart" peasants from the Russian and Austro-Hungarian empires became the source of intense controversy. Some Anglo-Canadian writers emphasized the great contribution which these central Europeans had made on their homesteads and in the many frontier work camps. Given the opportunity for Canadianization, these writers argued, Slavic, Jewish, and Italian immigrants would make fine citizens; they had much to offer once they had been assimilated.[24] In contrast, there was a wide body of literature which portrayed these "foreigners" as a long-term "problem" that would not be easily resolved. These Anglo-Canadian critics of the "open door" immigration policy emphasized that Canada had a limited capacity to absorb aliens from such different cultural backgrounds. They particularly criticized the perpetuation of bilingual schools in western Canada. The Great War intensified the debate, and many of the books and articles that appeared in these years were quite scurrilous; now central European immigrants were often referred to as "Huns" or as Bolshevik aliens.[25] Fortunately, most of this Anglo-Canadian xenophobia subsided in the early 1920s. With renewed immigration and the advent of the Great Depression there was a resumption of the argument that certain groups of European immigrants were a serious threat to Canadian society. Industrial unrest and communist activity were often blamed on radical aliens from eastern Europe. Canadians of German and Italian background were frequently charged with being pro-Nazi and pro-Fascist. But the most vicious attacks were directed toward another ethnic group – the Canadian Japanese community. Nor were there many voices raised in their defence. It was not until after 1945 that books and articles began to appear criticizing the federal government for its draconian treatment of these tragic victims of war.[26]

The post-war years also brought a reassessment of Canada's isolationist and uncharitable response to Jews and other refugees fleeing the Nazi terror.[27] This was paralleled by a resurgence of scholarly interest in the ethnic dimension of Canadian society. Again, most of the works were written from an Anglo-Canadian perspective, and there was sometimes a tendency to consider the immigrant as a "social problem."[28] But an encouraging development was the increasing number of books and articles that were written from the viewpoint of particular ethnic groups. Although many of these ethnic histories were too narrow in their focus, and ethnocentric rather than scholarly, it was nevertheless a beginning.[29] Another important trend was the growing number of scholarly works emanating from professional historians, sociologists, and political scientists. John Porter's *The Vertical Mosaic* (Toronto: University of Toronto Press 1965) was the most outstanding example of this new interdisciplinary approach. Increasingly, concepts such as the vertical mosaic, institutional completeness, ethnic enclosure, and ethnic identity would be utilized by a wide range of scholars involved in ethnic studies.[30] During the 1960s there was also a tendency to consider the English-Canadian and French-Canadian experience within the framework of the new ethnic studies. The publication of the *Report of the Royal Commission on Bilingualism and Biculturalism* in 1969 was a major step in this process. The October, 1971, commitment of the Trudeau government to multiculturalism and the subsequent creation of the Multiculturalism Directorate confirmed the fact that ethnic studies had arrived in Canada.[31]

American ethnic studies, which had been a thriving field of scholarly endeavour during the 1960s, strongly influenced many Canadian scholars. In the United States there had long been a prestigious tradition of ethnic history, sociology, and anthropology. Historians such as Marcus Lee Hansen and Oscar Handlin, sociologists such as Robert Park and Everett Hughes, and anthropologists such as Herbert Gans, Thomas Znaniecki, and Florian Znaniecki had made American ethnic studies a legitimate, if not an overly popular, field of scholarly endeavour.[32] During the 1960s, the black civil-rights movement and the growing awareness of the ethnic dimension of American society had a powerful impact on American scholars. By the end of the decade, a rich body of literature questioned many of the previous generalizations. For example, one component of this "new" ethnic history challenged the concept of the American "melting pot": did it create uniformity, or did it allow for diversity? Perhaps the most effective attempt to answer these questions was Milton Gordon's book *Assimilation in American Life: The Role of Race, Religion and National Origins* (New York: Oxford University Press 1964), in which he summarized the three contending ideologies of ethnic group relations: Anglo-conformity, the melting pot, and cultural pluralism.[33] Studies of immigration policy and nativism were another important area of inquiry which sought to redefine the role of ethnicity in American life. For example, John Higham, in his controversial *Strangers in the Land: Patterns of American Nativism* (New York: Atheneum 1963), defined nativism as a form of American nationalism composed of three major ideologies: xenophobia, anti-Catholicism, and anti-radicalism.[34]

Books on particular ethnic groups which emphasized both their Old World cultural background and their American experience also appeared in ever-growing numbers. These ethnic biographies were effectively complemented by a variety of topical studies: immigrants and the American labour movement; immigrant communities and the American city; ethnic cultures and American social institutions. The scope of American ethnic studies was further expanded during the 1970s, and by the end of the decade virtually thousands of articles and books had been published on this subject.

Publications in Canadian Ethnic Studies,
1970–1988

Canadian ethnic studies has been greatly affected by the voluminous and imaginative work of American scholars. During the 1960s and 1970s, many concepts and methodologies were borrowed from American literature and applied to the Canadian experience. For example, one can detect the influence of Milton Gordon and Nathan Glazer in the work of sociologists John Porter, W.W. Isajiw, and Alan Anderson. Historians have likewise demonstrated an eagerness to draw on American scholarship. This tendency has been most pronounced in studies that have emphasized the involvement of immigrant workers in the Canadian labour movement and those which have analyzed ethnic identity and group interaction. There have even been attempts to apply John Higham's nativist model to the Canadian ethnic and national situation, despite the obvious differences between the political and social cultures of the two nations.

Within Canada, other factors facilitated extensive research and publication activity in multiculturalism studies. One of these has been the availability of sources. The National Archives of Canada, the various provincial archives, and private organizations such as the Canadian Ukrainian Institute and the Multicultural History Society of Ontario have amassed an impressive collection of immigration and ethnic manuscript material. The latter two organizations have also sponsored several successful conferences and published a number of valuable books and periodicals. In this work they have been greatly assisted by the Jewish Historical Society of Canada, the Canadian Asian Studies Association, the Mennonite Historical Society of Canada, the Central and East European Studies Association of Canada, and, most notably, the Canadian Ethnic Studies Association and its journal, *Canadian Ethnic Studies*. Many scholarly journals have also shown considerable interest in publishing imaginative articles on Canadian ethnic studies. These include the *Journal of Folklore Studies, Multiculturalism, Canadian-American Review of Hungarian Studies, Polyphony, The Jewish Historical Society of Canada Journal*, and *Asianadian*. Equally encouraging has been the growing interest demonstrated by broader-based journals such as the *Canadian Review of Sociology and Anthropology, The Journal of Canadian Studies, Social History/Histoire sociale, Labour/Le Travail*, and the *Canadian Historical Review*. In 1980, the Canadian Historical Association initiated the publication of a booklet series on Canada's ethnic groups.[35] An even more ambitious project has been the Generation Series of ethnic biographies sponsored by the Multicultural Directorate. However, the actual selection of authors and the quality control have, until recently, primarily been the responsibility of the Ethnic Histories Advisory Panel. While some "experts" have maligned the Series, each of the specific studies has made a useful contribution to ethnic studies in Canada.[36]

Critique of the Major Studies

It is difficult to categorize precisely the various monographs and texts on ethnic studies that have appeared during the past eighteen years. The following units are, therefore, only tentative groupings, and many of these books could be placed under several headings. For each section, at least one major study has been selected for particular praise and recommendation. (See the select bibliography at the end of this chapter.)

General works. Although there are a considerable number of first-rate overview accounts, the most comprehensive treatment of the subject is Alan Anderson and James Frideres, *Ethnicity in Canada: Theoretical Perspectives* (Toronto: Butterworths 1981). This work combines a challenging theoretical perspective with a wide range of historical and sociological examples.

Multiculturalism and Canadian society. For the general reader and the specialist alike, the book by Robert Harney and Harold Troper, *Immigrants: A Portrait of the Urban Experience, 1890–1930* (Toronto: Van Nostrant & Reinhold 1975), on the urban experience of European immigrants in Toronto prior to 1930, offers many useful features. The excellent illustrations are effectively complemented by revealing recollections and historical analysis.

Racism and discrimination. Peter Ward's *White Canada Forever* (Montreal: McGill-Queen's University Press 1978), while restricted to an analysis of conditions in British Columbia, provides a lively and provocative discussion of the concepts of Anglo-Canadian xenophobia and cultural accommodation in the period 1871–1950.

Immigration, ethnicity, and the labour movement. In this category it is difficult to isolate one seminal work, since the number of useful studies is so extensive. But probably the most comprehensive treatment is provided in the anthology edited by Jorgen Dahlie and Tissa Fernando, *Ethnicity, Power & Politics in Canada* (Toronto: Methuen 1981), which contains articles by many of the leading ethnic scholars in Canada.

Visible minorities. Again, there is a range of excellent books. However, from a historical perspective the two most complete studies are Edgar Wickberg et al., *From China to Canada: A History of the Chinese Communities in Canada* (Toronto: McClelland and Stewart 1982), and Robin Wink's lengthy tome *The Blacks in Canada* (Montreal: McGill-Queens University Press 1971).

British immigrants. Donald Akenson's book *The Irish in Ontario: A Study in Rural History* (Kingston: McGill-Queen's University Press 1984), is the most challenging and thorough historical analysis in this category. He does, however, have strong competition from J.M. Bumsted (*The People's Clearance: Highland Emigration to British North America, 1770–1815,* Winnipeg: University of Manitoba Press 1982) and Joy Parr (*Labouring Children: British Immigrant Apprentices to Canada, 1869–1924,* Montreal: McGill-Queen's University Press 1980).

European immigrants. Because of the large number of books in this section, and the complexity of the different ethnic experiences, it is necessary to suggest a number of works. Some of the more outstanding are Manoly Lupul, ed., *A Heritage in Transition*; Bruno Ramirez, *Les Premiers Italiens de Montréal. L'origine de la Petite Italie du Québec* (Montreal: Boréal Express 1984); Anthony Rasporich, *For a Better Life: History of the Croatians in Canada* (Toronto: McClelland and Stewart 1982); and N.F. Dreisziger et al., *The Hungarian-Canadian Experience.* (See note 36 for full bibliographic information on the works by Lupul and Dreisziger.) These books go far beyond an ethnic biography; they develop a range of valuable insights into both the specific ethnic communities and their pattern of interaction with Canadian society.

Ethnoreligious immigrants. Although the number of books is not as extensive as in other sections, the quality is unusually high. Frank Epp's *Mennonites in Canada 1920: A People's Struggle for Survival* (Toronto: Macmillan 1982) and Irving Abella and Harold Troper, *None is too Many* (Toronto: Lester & Orpen Dennys 1982) are the best of a good sample.

Immigrant women. One of the most outstanding examples of work on this subject is Varpu Lindstrom-Best's *Defiant Sisters: A Social History of Finnish Immigrant Women in Canada* (Toronto: Multicultural Society of Toronto 1988). Based on her doctoral dissertation, Dr. Lindstrom-Best provides a thoroughly researched, well-written, and comprehensive analysis of Finnish immigrant women and their communities, with an emphasis on both their Old World background and their Canadian experience. Journals such as *Canadian Women's Studies* have also turned their attention to the experience of immigrant women, as was evident in the summer, 1988, issue entitled "Nordic Women."

The Writing of Ethnic Studies in Quebec

The field of ethnic studies has only recently made its appearance in the scholarly landscape of Francophone Quebec. As recently as 1983, the author of the most comprehensive survey of the literature produced in this field lamented the lack of a theoretical tradition capable of accounting for the place of ethnic phenomena within Quebec society. The major causes for this late development are to be found in the political and cultural conjuncture that has marked Francophone Quebec, to which we referred above. This is not to say, however, that empirical investigations of immigration and ethnic communities have been nonexistent. However, the timing of their appearance and the orientations they have expressed have largely been a function of the political and cultural preoccupations of the French-Canadian elites. Thus, it is not surprising if the earliest stimulus for such investigations came from the provincial government, and reflected a concern with the place and status of Francophone Quebec in the context of the rapid socio-economic transformations set off by the massive wave of post-war immigration.

As in most of the other provinces of Canada, problems growing out of the integration of immigrants into the host society were foremost on the agenda of Francophone researchers. The distinctive feature of their studies was that the integration process was placed within the context of a bicultural and bilingual host society such as Quebec's. Thus, prominent within this line of investigation were inquiries into the linguistic behaviour of ethnocultural minorities in an attempt to establish how trends in acculturation were likely to affect the demographic position of Francophones within Quebec society.

Another important trend in the development of ethnic studies – though by no means peculiar to Quebec – was seen in studies of specific ethnocultural communities undertaken by authors who were members of those communities. Some of the most important works attempting a comprehensive study of a given community fell into this category, and involved communities such as the Haitians, the Portuguese, the Greeks, and the Italians.[37] Like the government-sponsored investigations mentioned earlier, most of these latter works have tended to focus on the post-war wave of immigration, with their authors being mainly concerned with studying the process of integration that immigrants have experienced in Quebec.

While this crop of literature has produced, and analyzed, important data of a socio-economic and linguistic nature, relatively little progress has been made in comprehending the cultural and historical dimensions of ethnic communities. Some corrective tendencies, however, seem to be emerging from recent research projects. Researchers associated with the Centre d'études caraïbes, for instance, are reconstituting several immigration movements from the Caribbean islands and Central America, using both quantitative and qualitative data, and adopting a migration-study approach that assigns a central role to the immigrants' cultural background.[38] Similarly, a Laval University anthropologist, Mikhael Elbaz, is well advanced on a comprehensive and multidisciplinary project that investigates the ethnic and spatial segregation of Montreal's Jews, with a major emphasis placed on the role of cultural and ideological factors. Researchers at the Institut québecois de recherche sur la culture have undertaken studies on the Chinese[39] and the Arabs of Quebec that stress the centrality of culture in the development of those communities.

Despite the late development of ethnic studies in Francophone Quebec and the particular orientations that have characterized them, by the early 1980s the "ethnic issue" had definitely entered the agenda of most social-science disciplines, stimulating a growing scholarly production flowing from a variety of theoretical approaches. Conspicuous in this new scientific scenario, however, is the relative absence of systematic research on the immigration and ethnic history of the province. Here, too, it must be said that historians in Francophone Quebec have, perhaps more than members of any other scholarly profession, been absorbed into the ongoing political debate commonly known as "la question nationale." The prominent place traditionally assigned to institutional history, economic history, and the history of ideologies has necessarily resulted in a neglect for groups within Quebec society that were considered external to the process of national self-assertion.

The recent attention that has been given to immigration and ethnic history may be explained, on the one hand, by the ethnic affiliation of the researchers involved, and, on the other hand, by the important development of the "new social history" in North America and the growing importance of immigration history in that development. Factors such as these are behind the historical research that has been progressing on the Italians, the Chinese, and the North African Jews, as well as the growing sensitivity that some Quebec urban historians are manifesting toward ethnic phenomena.[40]

CONCLUSION
ETHNIC STUDIES IN CANADA
DURING THE NEXT DECADE:
POSSIBLE DIRECTIONS

Although it is difficult to predict the exact direction ethnic studies in Canada will follow during the next ten years, there are several questions that should be considered. One of these is whether the federal government and the provincial authorities will continue the high level of financial support sustained over the previous decade. In the spring of 1986, the minister responsible for multiculturalism announced that a much more pragmatic approach would hitherto be adopted toward ethnic studies by his department: "Multiculturalism policy in the past tended to dwell primarily on folklore and pride in cultural tradition. As a new Canadian myself, I saw this focus as useful and important but, nevertheless, limiting. The day is long gone when the 'Celebrate Our Differences' approach to multiculturalism was enough." Instead, he urged Canadians, "enhanced opportunities in small business and international trade will help us make complete and appropriate use of our multicultural resources and develop the markets they can help us reach."[41] However, in July of 1988 the Mulroney government moved away from this rather narrow multicultural mandate. With the passage of Bill C-93 (The Multicultural Act), the Mulroney government created a new ministry with commitments to:

3 (a) recognize the understanding that multiculturalism reflects the cultural and racial diversity of Canadian society and acknowledges the freedom of all members of Canadian society to preserve, enhance and share their cultural heritage ...

(c) promote full and equitable participation of individuals and communities in the continuing evolution and shaping of all aspects of Canadian society and assist them in the elimination of any barrier to such participation ...

(f) encourage and assist the social, cultural and political institutions of Canada to be both respectful and inclusive of Canada's multicultural character ...

(h) foster the recognition and appreciation of the diverse cultures of Canadian society and promote the reflection and the evolving expression of those cultures;

(i) preserve and enhance the use of languages other then English and French while strengthening the status and use of the official languages of Canada ...[42]

Obviously, the policies that the federal government adopts toward multiculturalism will continue to have an important impact on ethnic studies in Canada. But in addition, there are important conceptual issues which need to be confronted in order to enhance future ethnic-studies publications. One of the most fundamental questions is the viability of studying ethnic identity as a sociological phenomenon in Canada. In a provocative 1983 article, Roberto Perin argued that

non-British, non-French groups in Canada did not meet the standard
criteria utilized in defining European ethnic groups:

An ethnic culture cannot survive simply on memories of a distant space.
To maintain its distinctiveness and to flourish, it must interact with a real,
an immanent space. In North America, however, immigrant groups do not
have a space they can claim exclusively for themselves. They are dispersed
across a continent and must contend with the ever-encroaching presence
of the receiving culture.[43]

Not surprisingly, many ethnic scholars do not accept Perin's arguments, and argue that European models do not necessarily apply
to the North American situation. This debate over the "right" kind
of ethnic studies brings us back to the starting point of this essay –
the fragmentation of the field into many different "schools" and
disciplines. Whether this is a problem or an asset remains to be
determined. What is more obvious is that during the past fifteen
years ethnic studies in Canada has enjoyed remarkable growth.

NOTES

1 Alan Anderson and James Frideres, *Ethnicity in Canada: Theoretical Perspectives* (Toronto: Butterworths 1981), 6.

2 Alan Anderson, "Canadian Ethnic Studies and New Direction," *Journal of Canadian Studies* 17, no. 1 (Spring 1982): 5–14, quoted 5. In this
special edition on multiculturalism the *Journal* published other useful
articles: Norman Buchignani, "Canadian Ethnic Research and Multiculturalism"; Freda Hawkins, "Multiculturalism in Two Countries: The
Canadian and Australian Experience"; Rudolf Kalin and J.W. Berry,
"Canadian Ethnic Attitudes and Identity in the Context of National
Unity"; Evelyn Kallen, "Multiculturalism: Ideology, Policy and Reality"; Manoly Lupul, "The Political Implementation of Multiculturalism"; Howard Palmer, "Canadian Immigration and Ethnic History in
the 1970s and 1980s"; Anthony Richmond, "Canadian Unemployment
and the Threat to Multiculturalism"; Lionel Rubinoff, "Multiculturalism and the Metaphysics of Pluralism"; and Victor Ujimoto, "Visible
Minorities and Multiculturalism: Planned Social Change Strategies for
the Next Decade."

3 Anderson and Frideres, *Ethnicity in Canada*, 273.

4 The Journal of CESA, *Canadian Ethnic Studies*, has been published since
the early 1970s. It now appears four times a year with a diverse collection of articles, research notes, and book reviews, reflecting CESA's

commitment to the interdisciplinary approach to ethnic studies. Particularly useful are the special thematic editions, including "Ethnic Radicals," 10, no. 2 (1978); "Ukrainians in the Canadian City," 12, no. 2 (1980); "Ethnicity and Feminity," 13, no. 1 (1981); and "Ethnic Art and Architecture," 16, no. 3 (1984).

5 The Canadian Centre for Folk Culture encourages ethnic studies in several ways. It works closely with the ethnic archives section, National Archives (Ottawa), in collecting various cultural materials relating to different ethnic groups. It also publishes useful monographs on different ethnic groups. For example: Ban Seng Hoe, *Structural Changes of Two Chinese Communities in Alberta, Canada* (1976); Robert Klymasz, *Folk Narrative Among Ukrainian Canadians In Western Canada* (1973); G. James Patterson, *The Roumanians of Saskatchewan: Four Generations of Adaptation* (1977); Matt Salo and Sheila Salo, *The Kalderas in Eastern Canada* (1977); Charles Sutyla, *The Finnish Sauna in Manitoba* (1977); Koozma Tarasoff, *Traditional Doukhobor Folkways: An Ethnographic and Biographical Record of Prescribed Behaviour* (1977); Jan Harold Brunvand, *Norwegian Settlers in Alberta* (1974).

6 Other government agencies offering multicultural services include the Ministry of the Attorney General, the Ministry of Consumer and Commercial Relations, the Ministry of Labour, the Secretariat for Social Development, TV Ontario, and the Ontario Human Rights Commission.

7 There have been three monographs in the Ethnic and Immigration History Series: Milda Danys, *DP: Lithuanian Immigration to Canada after the Second World War* (1984); Robert Harney, *Gathering Place: Peoples and Neighbourhoods of Toronto, 1834–1945* (1985); and Varpu Lindstrom-Best, *Defiant Sisters: A Social History of Finnish Women in Canada* (1988).

8 The York University Ethnic Research Programme has published a number of useful studies. The Centre for Urban and Community Studies (University of Toronto) has also conducted a number of important survey studies. Ethnic studies at the University of Toronto was given further encouragement in 1984 with the endowment of the Chair of Ukrainian Studies.

9 The University of Ottawa also has a Chair of Celtic Studies. Carleton University has established a liaison with the University of Copenhagen in order to encourage Scandinavian studies in Canada.

10 Other forms of support in Ontario include the Chinese-Canadian Fellowship at the University of Toronto, the Mohawk College (Hamilton) Multicultural Interaction Project, and the Certificate Program in Canadian Cross Cultural Studies at Ryerson College.

11 Manitoba also hosts three major ethnocultural folk festivals annually: Folkorama (Winnipeg), the Icelandic Festival (Gimli), and the National

Ukrainian Festival (Dauphin). These and other cultural activities in the province are co-ordinated by Manitoba's Intercultural Council.

12 The Mennonite Heritage Centre is the creation of the Mennonite Historical Society, which was formally created in 1953. This organization was also responsible for the establishment of the Mennonite Village Museum located near Steinback.

13 The Ukrainian Archives, or *Oseredok*, is the largest Ukrainian cultural resource centre and repository of Ukrainian historical and cultural artifacts in North America. The creation of the Centre for Ukrainian Studies at St. Andrew's College, University of Manitoba, during the late 1970s was another factor in the further development of ethnic studies in the province.

14 The Canadian Institute for Ukrainian Studies was established in 1976 as a national institution to meet the academic needs of Ukrainians in Canada. It has four major objectives: to encourage program development in Ukrainian studies at the undergraduate and graduate level; to serve as a resource centre for English-Ukrainian bilingual education; to encourage and co-ordinate research and publications in Ukrainian studies; and to encourage contacts among scholars and students in Ukrainian studies through seminars and conferences. Two of the more useful publications of the Institute are Frances Swyripa, *Ukrainian Canadians: a survey of their portrayal in English-language works* (1978), and Frances Swypira and John Thompson, *Loyalties in Conflict* (1982).

15 In British Columbia, ethnic studies covers a wide range of subjects: native people, European immigrants, and Asian immigrants. The cultural history and characteristics of Chinese, Japanese, East Indians, and Southern Asians are the mandate of private centres such as the Chinese Cultural Centre, the Asia Pacific Foundation of Canada (Vancouver), and the Institute of Asian Research at the University of British Columbia. At UBC there is also an interdisciplinary Committee on Ethnic Studies. Simon Fraser University established in 1984 a Credit Diploma Program in Ethnic Relations focusing on the study of ethnically defined conflicts and problems of migration. Many of the students in this program are in human-service professions – police officers, social workers, teachers, journalists, health practitioners, and so on.

16 In 1975, the Beaton Institute was established as part of the College of Cape Breton to be a centre of research into the culture and historical development of the region. St. Mary's College, Halifax, also became very much involved in ethnic studies, and in 1981 hosted the very successful conference "Ethnic Identity in Atlantic Canada." In addition, the Multicultural Association of Nova Scotia has been active in increasing the public awareness of ethnic studies in the province and

as a vehicle of communication between those involved in ethnic studies. In New Brunswick, the Multicultural Council was created in 1983 to achieve greater public and government recognition of the province's multicultural nature. In 1983, St. Francis Xavier University was provided with an endowment by the Multicultural Directorate for the establishment of a Chair in Gaelic Studies. The formation of the Irish Canadian Cultural Association of New Brunswick further enhanced Celtic studies in the Atlantic region.

17 The study of Acadian culture in New Brunswick was further enhanced by the endowment of the Chair in Acadian Studies at the University of Moncton.

18 David Rome, Judith Nefsky, and Paule Obermeir, *Les Juifs du Québec. Bibliographie rétrospective annotée* (Quebec City 1981); Gary Caldwell and Éric Waddell, dirs., *Les anglophones du Québec: de majoritaires à minoritaires* (Quebec City 1982); Gary Caldwell, *Les études ethniques au Québec – Bilan et perspectives* (Quebec City 1983); Tina Ioannou, *La communauté grecque du Québec* (Quebec City 1984); Pierre Anctil and Gary Caldwell, eds., *Juifs et réalités juives au Québec* (Quebec City 1984); Ronald Rudin, *The Forgotten Quebecers. A History of English-Speaking Quebec, 1759–1980* (Quebec City 1985). See also the special issue of the Institut's journal *Questions de culture*: "Migrations et communautés culturelles," 2 (1982).

19 Francois-Xavier Garneau, *Histoire du Canada*, 4 vols. (Quebec City: Imp. de N. Aubin 1845–52); Jean-B.A. Ferland, *Cours d'histoire du Canada*, 2 vols. (Quebec City: 1861); Thomas Chapais, *Cours d'histoire du Canada*, 4 vols. (Quebec City: J.-P Garneau 1919–34); Abbé Lionel Groulx, *Histoire du Canada français depuis la découverte* (Montreal 1960) and *Le Canada français missionnaire: une autre grande aventure* (Montreal: Fides 1962).

20 Egerton Ryerson, *The Loyalists of America and Their Times* (Toronto: W. Briggs 1880); William Coffin, *1812: The War and Its Moral: A Canadian Chronicle* (Montreal: J. Lovell 1864); J.G. Bourinot, *Canada Under British Rule, 1760–1900* (Cambridge: Cambridge University Press 1909); J.S. Willison, *Anglo-Saxon Amity* (Toronto 1906); Francis Parkman, *Montcalm and Wolfe* (Boston: Little, Brown 1884); G.M. Wrong, *The Canadians: The Story of a People* (Toronto: University of Toronto Press 1938); Chester Martin, *Foundations of Canadian Nationhood* (Toronto: University of Toronto Press 1938); R.G. Trotter, *Canadian Federation: Its Origin and Achievement: A Study in Nation Building* (Toronto: Dent 1924); Carl Berger, *The Sense of Power: Studies in the Ideas of Canadian Imperialism, 1867–1914* (Toronto: University of Toronto Press 1970).

21 Books that tended to deprecate the merit of native Canadians include John McLean's *The Indians of Canada: Their Manners and Customs* (Toronto: William Briggs 1899) and George MacDonald, *British Columbia*

and Vancouver Island [...] (London: Longman, Green 1862). Although French Canadians fared much better from Anglo-Canadian writers, there was nevertheless a strong tendency to minimize the cultural vitality of French-Canadian society and to suggest that its culture was both hierarchical and static. Examples include J.M. McMullen, *The History of Canada from its Discovery to the Present Time* (Brockville, Ont.: McMullen 1891); Byron Nicholson, *The French Canadians: A Sketch of His More Prominent Characteristics* (Toronto: Bryant Press 1902); G.M. Grant, *French Canadian Life and Character* (Toronto: A. Belford & Co. 1899); and D.G. Creighton, *The Commercial Empire of the St. Lawrence, 1760–1850* (Toronto: Ryerson 1937).

22 Some of the more critical studies of Irish immigration included W. Bridges, *Ireland and America* (London: 1847), and Anthony Bimba, *The Molly McGuires* (New York: International Publishers 1932).

23 Helen Cowan, *British Emigration to British North America* (Toronto: University of Toronto Press 1961); Norman Macdonald, *Canada, Immigration and Colonization, 1841–1903* (Toronto: Macmillan 1966); Rudolph Vecoli, "European Americans: From Immigrants to Ethnics," *International Migration Review* 6, no. 4 (Winter 1972): 403–34.

24 Some of the more sympathetic studies written from the Anglo-Canadian perspective were Edmund Bradwin, *The Bunkhouse Man* (Toronto: University of Toronto Press 1928); J.W. Dafoe, *Clifford Sifton and His Times* (Toronto: Macmillan 1931); Alfred Fitzpatrick, *The University in Overalls: A Plea for Part-time Study* (Toronto: Press of the Hunter Rose Co. 1920); C.A. Dawson, "Group Settlement: Ethnic Communities in Western Canada," in W.A. Mackintosh and W.L.G. Joerg, eds., *Canadian Frontiers of Settlement Series*, vol. 7 (Toronto: Macmillan 1936); Robert England, *The Central European Immigrant in Canada* (Toronto: Macmillan 1929); and *The Colonization of Western Canada* (London: P.S. King 1936); Kate Foster, *Our Canadian Mosaic* (Toronto: Dominion Council, YMCA 1926); Dr. R.P. Bryce, *The Value to Canada of the Continental Immigrant* (Toronto: 1928); W.G. Smith, *Building the Nation* (Toronto: Canada Congregational Missionary Society 1922); Arthur Morton, *History of Prairie Settlement* (Toronto: Macmillan 1968); John Murray Gibbon, *Canadian Mosaic* (Toronto: McClelland and Stewart 1938); and Charles Young, *The Ukrainian Canadians: A Study in Assimilation* (Toronto: T. Nelson 1931).

25 There was also an appreciable body of literature which stressed the social problems of European immigration. Some of the major works are J.T.M. Anderson, *The Education of the New Canadian* (London: Dent 1918); W. Bridgman, *Breaking Prairie Sod* (Toronto: Musson Book Co. 1920); J.S. Woodsworth, *Strangers Within Our Gates* (Toronto: F.C. Stephenson 1909); *My Neighbour* (Toronto: Missionary Society of the

Methodist Church 1911); and Charles Magrath, *Canada's Growth and Some Problems Affecting It* (Ottawa: Mortimer Press 1910).

26 Books dealing with immigrants from Asia ranged from sympathetic studies, such as C.H. Young and H.R.Y. Reid, *The Japanese Canadians* (Toronto: University of Toronto Press 1938), and C.J. Woodsworth, *Canada and the Orient* (Toronto: Macmillan 1941), to polemics such as H. Glynn-Ward, *The Writing on the Wall* (Vancouver: Sun Publishing 1921), and F. Leighton Thomas, *Japan: the Octopus of the East and Its Menace to Canada* (Vancouver: 1932). There were, however, important books written from the perspective of these ethnic groups themselves, such as Cheng Tien-Fang's *Oriental Immigration in Canada* (Shanghai: Commercial Press 1931). One of the most important of the liberal revisionist studies was by the sociologist Forrest LaViolette, *The Canadian Japanese and World War II: A Sociological and Psychological Account* (Toronto: University of Toronto Press 1948).

27 Simon Belkin, *Through Narrow Gates: A Review of Jewish Immigration, Colonization and Immigrant Aid Work in Canada 1840–1940* (Montreal: Canadian Jewish Congress 1966); Joseph Kage, ed., *With Faith and Thanksgiving: The Story of Two Hundred Years of Jewish Immigration and Immigrant Aid Effort in Canada, 1760–1960* (Montreal: Eagle 1962).

28 David Corbett, *Canada's Immigration Policy: A Critique* (Toronto: University of Toronto Press 1957); Julian Park, ed., *The Culture of Contemporary Canada* (Ithaca, NY: Cornell University Press 1957); Harry Hawthorn, ed., *The Doukhobors of British Columbia* (Vancouver: University of British Columbia 1955); Peter Russell, ed., *Nationalism in Canada* (Toronto: McGraw-Hill 1966); Anthony Richmond, *Post-War Immigrants in Canada* (Toronto: University of Toronto Press 1967); J.F.C. Wright, *Slava Bohu: The Story of the Doukhobors* (New York: Farrar and Rinehart 1940); Arthur Chiel, *The Jews of Manitoba* (Toronto: University of Toronto Press 1961).

29 John Gellner and John Smerek, *The Czechs and Slovaks in Canada* (Toronto: University of Toronto Press 1968); David Rome, ed., *Jews in Canadian Literature* (Montreal: Bronfman Collection 1970); Vladimir Kaye, *Early Ukrainian Settlements in Canada, 1895–1900* (Toronto: University of Toronto Press 1964); J.M. Kirschbaum, *Slovaks in Canada* (Toronto: Canadian Ethnic Press Association 1967); John Kosa, *Land of Choice: The Hungarians in Canada* (Toronto: University of Toronto Press 1957); W.J. Lindal, *The Icelanders in Canada* (Ottawa: National Publishers 1967); Vera Lysenko, *Men in Sheepskin Coats: A Study of Assimilation* (Toronto: Ryerson Press 1947); B.G. Sack, *History of the Jews in Canada* (Montreal: Harvest House 1965); Antonio Spada, *The Italians in Canada* (Ottawa: Riviera Publishing Co. 1969); Victor Turek, *Poles in Manitoba* (Toronto: Polish Research Institute in Canada 1967); *The Polish-Language Press in*

Canada: Its History and a Biographical Sketch (Toronto: Polish Alliance Press 1962); O. Woycenko, *The Ukrainians in Canada* (Ottawa: Trident Press 1967); Paul Yuzyk, *The Ukrainians in Manitoba: A Social History* (Toronto: University of Toronto Press 1953). The proceedings of the National Conferences on Canadian Slavs in 1966 and 1969 also contained some useful articles.

30 Two broader studies that demonstrated this new social-science approach were Anthony Richmond, *Immigrants and Ethnic Groups in Metropolitan Toronto: A Preliminary Study* (Toronto: Institute for Behavioural Research, York University 1967), and Freda Hawkins, *Canada and Immigration* (Montreal: McGill-Queen's University Press 1972).

31 The Royal Commission on Bilingualism and Biculturalism commissioned a number of specialized multidisciplinary studies on various aspects of ethnicity. Some of the more notable were Jeremy Boissevain, *The Italians of Montreal: Social Adjustment in a Plural Society* (Ottawa: Queen's Printer 1970) and four reports that are available on microfiche: R.F. Aide, "The Ethnic Press"; M.S. Donnelly, "Ethnic Participation in Municipal Government – Winnipeg, St. Boniface and the Metropolitan Corporation of Great Winnipeg"; Foon Sien, "The Chinese in Canada"; and Saul Frankel, "Political Orientation and Ethnicity in a Bicultural Society." The interdisciplinary approach was also effectively utilized in the study of Canada's major ethnoreligious groups. Examples include E.K. Francis, *In Search of Utopia: The Mennonites of Manitoba* (Glencoe, Ill.: Free Press 1955); George Woodcock and Ivan Avakumovic, *The Doukhobors* (Toronto: Oxford University Press 1968); and Victor Peters, *All Things Common* (Minneapolis: University of Minnesota Press 1965).

32 Marcus Lee Hansen, *The Atlantic Migration, 1607–1860: A History of Continuing Settlement of the United States* (New York: Harper & Row 1961); Oscar Handlin, *Boston's Immigrants: A Study in Acculturation* (Cambridge: Belknap 1941); Robert Park, *The Immigrant Press and Its Control* (New York: Harper 1922); Everett Hughes, *French Canada in Transition* (Toronto: Gage 1943); H. Gans, *The Urban Villagers: Group and Class in the Life of Italian Americans* (New York: Free Press of Glencoe 1962); William Thomas and Florian Znaniecki, *The Polish Peasant in Europe and America*, 2 vols. (New York: Knopf 1927).

33 See also Will Herberg, *Protestant, Catholic, Jew* (New York: Anchor Books 1960); Nathan Glazer and Daniel Moynihan, *Beyond the Melting Pot* (Cambridge: MIT Press 1963); and Joshua Fishman et al., *Language Loyalty in the United States* (The Hague: Mouton 1966).

34 See also Maldwyn Allen Jones, *American Immigration* (Chicago: University of Chicagao Press 1960); Philip Taylor, *The Distant Magnet: Euro-*

pean Emigration to the U.S.A. (London: Eyre and Spottiswoode 1971);
Robert Murray, *Red Scare: A Study in National Hysteria* (Minneapolis:
University of Minnesota Press 1955).

35 By 1986 the following titles had appeared: D. Avery and J. Federo-
witz, *The Poles*; J.M. Bumsted, *The Scots*; O.W. Gerus and J.E. Rea, *The
Ukrainians*; David Higgs, *The Portuguese*; Hugh Johnston, *The East Indi-
ans*; Varpu Lindstrom-Best, *The Finns*; K.M. Mclaughlin, *The Germans*;
Jin Tan and Pat Roy, *The Chinese*; Bernard Vigod, *The Jews*; James
Walker, *The West Indians*; and W. Peter Ward, *The Japanese*.

36 By 1986 ten volumes had been published: Karl Aun, *The Political Refugees: A History of the Estonians in Canada* (Toronto: McClelland and
Stewart 1986); Norman Buchignani and Doreen Indra, with Ram Svi-
vastava, *Continuous Journey: A Social History of South Asians in Canada*
(Toronto: McClelland and Stewart 1986); Baha Abu-Luban, *An Olive
Branch on the Family Tree: The Arabs in Canada* (Toronto: McClelland
and Stewart 1980); Peter Chimbos, *The Canadian Odyssey: The Greek Experience in Canada* (Toronto: McClelland and Stewart 1980); Gulbrand
Loken, *From Fiord to Frontier: A History of the Norwegians in Canada* (To-
ronto: McClelland and Stewart 1980); N.F. Dreisziger et al., *Struggle
and Hope: The Hungarian-Canadian Experience* (Toronto: McClelland and
Stewart 1982); Manoly Lupul, ed., *A Heritage in Transition: Essays in the
History of Ukrainians in Canada* (Toronto: McClelland and Stewart
1982); Henry Radecki and Benedykt Heydenkorn, *A Member of a Dis-
tinguished Family: The Polish Group in Canada* (Toronto: McClelland and
Stewart 1976); Anthony Rasporich, *For a Better Life: A History of the
Croatians in Canada* (Toronto: McClelland and Stewart 1983); W. Stan-
ford Reid, *The Scottish Tradition in Canada* (Toronto: McClelland and
Stewart 1976); Edgar Wickberg et al., *From China to Canada: A History
of the Chinese Communities in Canada* (Toronto: McClelland and Stewart
1982).

37 P. Déjean, *Les Haïtiens au Québec* (Montreal: Les presses de l'Université
du Québec 1979); Stephanos Constantinides, *Les Grecs du Québec*
(Montreal: O. Metoikos-Le métèque 1983); Antonio J. Alphalhao and
Victor M.P. Da Rosa, *Les Portugais du Québec* (Ottawa: Éd. de l'Université d'Ottawa 1979).

38 Micheline Labelle, Geneviève Turcotte, Marianne Kempeneers, and
Deidre Meintel, *Histoires d'immigrées: itinéraires d'ouvrières Colombiennes,
Greques, Haïtiennes et Portugaises à Montréal* (Montreal: Boréal 1987).

39 Denise Helly, *Les Chinois à Montréal, 1877–1951* (Quebec City: Institut
québécois de recherche sur la culture 1987).

40 In addition to Helly, *Les Chinois à Montréal*, and Rudin, *The Forgotten
Quebecers*, see Sylvie Taschereau, *Pays et patries: mariages et lieux d'origine des Italiens de Montréal, 1906–1930* (Montreal: Études italiennes

no. 1, Université de Montréal 1987), and Bruno Ramirez, "La recherche sur les Italiens du Québec," *Questions de culture* 2 (1982): 103–12.
41 Canadian Ethnic Association *Bulletin* (Spring 1986): 1–2.
42 *The Canadian Gazette, Part III* (Statutes of Canada), November 1, 1988, chapter 31 (Ottawa: Supply and Services 1988): 3–4.
43 Roberto Perin, "Clio as an Ethnic: The Third Force in Canadian Historiography," *Canadian Historical Review*, no. 4 (1983): 443.

SELECT STUDIES PUBLISHED 1970–1988

General Works

Bienvenue, Rita and Jay Goldstein. *Ethnicity and Ethnic Relations in Canada*. Toronto: Butterworths 1985.

Broadfoot, Barry. *The Immigrant Years: From Europe to Canada, 1945–1967*. Vancouver: Douglas & McIntyre 1986.

Buchignani, Norman. *Cultures in Canada: Strength in Diversity*. Regina: Weigl Educational Publishers 1984.

Burnet, Jean with Howard Palmer. *Coming Canadians: An Introduction to a History of Canada's Peoples*. Toronto: McClelland & Stewart 1988.

Dreidger, L., ed. *The Canadian Ethnic Mosaic*. Toronto: McClelland & Stewart 1978.

– *Ethnic Canada: Identities and Inequalities*. Toronto: Copp Clark Pitman 1987.

Elliott, Jean, ed. *Two Nations, Many Cultures: Ethnic Groups in Canada*. Scarborough, Ont.: Prentice-Hall 1983.

Hughes, D.R. and E. Kallen. *The Anatomy of Racism*. Montreal: Harvest House 1974.

Isajiw, W.W., ed. *Identities: The Impact of Ethnicity on Canadian Society*. Toronto: Peter Martin Associates 1977.

Krauter, J.F. and M. Davis. *Minority Canadians: Ethnic Groups*. Toronto: Methuen 1978.

Migus, P.M., ed. *Sounds Canadian: Languages and Cultures in Multi-Ethnic Society*. Toronto: Peter Martin Associates 1975.

Montero, G. *The Immigrants*. Toronto: J. Lorimer 1977.

Palmer, Howard, ed. *Immigration and the Rise of Multiculturalism*. Vancouver: Copp Clark 1975.

Reitz, Jeffrey. *The Survival of Ethnic Groups*. Toronto: McGraw-Hill Ryerson 1980.

Wood, Dean. *Multicultural Canada: A Teacher's Guide to Ethnic Studies*. Toronto: OISE 1984.

Multiculturalism and Canadian Society

Balan, Jars, ed. *Identifications: Ethnicity and the Writer in Canada*. Edmonton: Canadian Institute of Ukrainian Studies 1982.

– ed. *Identifiers: Ethnicity and the Writer in Canada*. Edmonton: Canadian Institute of Ukrainian Studies 1986.

Bancroft, George. *The Novice and the Newcomer: Student Teacher's Perceptions on Multiculturalism and Education*. London, Ont.: Third Eye Publications 1981.

Berry, John and Michael La Ferriere, eds. *Multiculturalism in Canada: Social and Educational Perspectives*. Toronto: Allyn and Bacon 1984.

Breton, Albert & Raymond Breton. *Why Disunity? An Analysis of Linguistic and Regional Cleavages in Canada*. Montreal: Institute for Research on Public Policy 1978.

Bullivant, Brian. *The Pluralist Dilemma in Education: Six Case Studies*. Sydney: George Allen & Unwin 1981.

Cosper, Ronald. *Ethnicity and Occupation in Atlantic Canada: The Social and Economic Implications of Cultural Diversity*. Halifax: International Education Centre, Saint Mary's University 1984.

Danesi, Marcel. *Teaching a Heritage Language to Dialect-Speaking Students*. Toronto: OISE 1986.

Dorotich, Daniel, ed. *Education and Canadian Multiculturalism: Some Problems and Some Solutions*. Saskatoon: Canadian Society for the Study of Education 1981.

Driedger, Leo and Neena Chappell. *Aging and Ethnicity: Toward an Interface*. Toronto: Butterworths 1987.

Grey, Julius. *Immigration Law in Canada*. Scarborough, Ont.: Butterworths 1984.

Harney, Robert, ed. "Sports and Ethnicity." *Polyphony* (1985).

Isajiw, Wsevolod. *Socialization as a Factor in Ethnic Identity Retention*. Toronto: Centre for Urban and Community Studies, University of Toronto 1982.

Kovacs, Martin, ed. *Ethnic Canadians: Culture and Education*. Regina: Canadian Plains Research Centre 1978.

Mallea, John and Jonathan Young. *Cultural Diversity and Canadian Education: Issues and Innovations*. Ottawa: Carleton University Press 1984.

Mitges, Gus. *Multiculturalism: Building the Canadian Mosaic. (Report of the Standing Committee on Multiculturalism)*. Ottawa: Supply & Services Canada 1987.

Norris, John. *Strangers Entertained: A History of Ethnic Groups of British Columbia*. Vancouver: British Columbia Centennial '71 Committee 1971.

Sharpson, Stan et al., eds. *Bilingualism and Multiculturalism in Canadian Education*. Vancouver: Centre for the Study of Curriculum, University of British Columbia 1982.

Ward, W. Peter. *White Canada Forever: Popular Attitudes and Public Policy toward Orientals in British Columbia*. Montreal: McGill-Queen's University Press 1978.

Racism and Discrimination: General

Betcherman, Lita-Rose. *The Swastika and the Maple Leaf*. Toronto: Fitzhenry & Whiteside 1975.

Craig, Terrance. *Racial Attitudes in English-Canadian Fiction, 1905–1980*. Waterloo, Ont.: Wilfrid Laurier University Press 1986.

Fraser, Joyce. *Cry of the Illegal Immigrant*. Toronto: Williams-Wallace Productions International 1980.

Head, Wilson. *Adaptation of Immigrants: Perceptions of Ethnic and Racial Discrimination*. Toronto 1981.

Levitt, Cyril and William Shaffir. *The Riot at Christie Pits*. Toronto: Lester Orpen & Dennys 1987.

Palmer, Howard. *Patterns of Prejudice: A History of Nativism in Alberta*. Toronto: McClelland & Stewart 1982.

Wagner, Jonathan. *Brothers Beyond the Sea, National Socialism in Canada*. Waterloo, Ont.: Wilfrid Laurier University Press 1981.

Weinmann, Gabriel and Conrad Winn. *Hate on Trial: The Zundel Affairs, the Media and Public Opinion in Canada*. Oakville, Ont.: Mosaic Press 1986.

Immigration, Ethnicity, and the Labour Movement

Avery, Donald. *'Dangerous Foreigners': European Immigrant Workers and Labour Radicalism in Canada, 1896–1932*. Toronto: McClelland & Stewart 1979.

Bercuson, David. *Fools and Wisemen: The Rise and Fall of the Big Union*. Toronto: McGraw-Hill Ryerson 1978.

Copp, J. Terry. *Anatomy of Poverty: The Condition of the Working Class in Montreal, 1897–1929*. Toronto: McClelland & Stewart 1974.

Kealey, Gregory. *Toronto Workers Respond to Industrial Capitalism, 1867–1892*. Toronto: University of Toronto Press 1980.

Kolasky, John. *The Shattered Illusion: The History of the Ukrainian Pro-Communist Organizations in Canada*. Toronto: PMA Books 1979.

McCormack, A. Ross. *Reformers, Rebels and Revolutionaries*. Toronto: University of Toronto Press 1978.

Palmer, Bryan. *A Culture in Conflict: Skilled Workers and Industrial Capitalism in Hamilton, Ontario, 1860–1914*. Montreal: McGill-Queen's University Press 1979.

Potrebenko, Helen. *No Streets of Gold*. Vancouver: New Star Books 1977.

Ramirez, Bruno and Michael Del Balso. *The Italians of Montreal: From So-journing to Settlement*. Montreal: Éditions du Courant 1980.

Rasporich, Anthony. *For a Better Life: A History of the Croatians in Canada*. Toronto: McClelland & Stewart 1983.

There are also a number of useful articles in *Labour/Le Travail* and *Canadian Ethnic Studies* which combine ethnic and labour history.

Visible Minorities

Adachi, Ken. *The Enemy That Never Was*. Toronto: McClelland & Stewart 1976.

Adelman, Howard. *Canada and the Indo-Chinese Refugees*. Regina: L.A. Weigl Education Associates 1982.

Austin, Alvyn. *Saving China: Canadian Missionaries in the Middle Kingdom, 1888–1959*. Toronto: University of Toronto Press 1986.

Buchignani, Norman and Doreen Indra. *Continuous Journey: A Social History of South Asians in Canada*. Toronto: McClelland & Stewart 1985.

Chan, Anthony. *Gold Mountain: The Chinese in the New World*. Vancouver: New Star Books 1982.

Christiansen, J.M. et al. *West Indians in Toronto: Implications for Helping Professionals*. Toronto: Family Service Association of Metropolitan Toronto 1980.

Dorais, Louis-Jacques et al. *Les Vietnamiens du Québec: Profil sociolinguistique*. Quebec City: Centre international de recherche sur le bilinguisme 1984.

Elliott, Lorris, ed. *Other Voices: Writings by Blacks in Canada*. Toronto: Williams-Wallace 1985.

Halli, Shivalingappa. *How Minority Status Affects Fertility: Asian Groups in Canada*. New York: Greenwood Press 1987.

Head, Wilson. *The Black Presence in the Canadian Mosaic: A Study of Perception and the Practice of Discrimination Against Blacks in Metropolitan Toronto*. Toronto: Ontario Human Rights Commission 1975.

Henry, Keith. *Black Politics in Toronto Since World War I*. Toronto: Multicultural History Society of Ontario 1981.

Hill, Donna, ed. *A Black Man's Toronto, 1914–80*. Toronto: Multicultural History Society of Ontario 1981.

Johnston, Hugh. *The Voyage of the Komagata Maru: The Sikh Challenge to Canada's Color Bar*. Delhi: Oxford University Press 1979.

Kilian, Crawford. *Go Do Some Great Thing: The Black Pioneers of British Columbia*. Vancouver: Douglas & McIntyre 1978.

Magill, Dennis. *Nova Scotian Blacks: An Historical and Structural Overview*. Halifax: Institute of Public Affairs, Dalhousie University Press 1970.

Nakano, Takeo Ujo. *Within The Barbed Wire Fence: A Japanese Man's Account of His Internment in Canada*. Toronto: University of Toronto Press 1980.

Ramcharan, Subhas. *Racism: Non-Whites in Canada*. Toronto: Butterworths 1982.

Spray, W.A. *The Blacks in New Brunswick*. Fredericton: Brunswick Press 1972.

Sunahara, A. *The Politics of Racism: The Uprooting of the Japanese Canadians During the Second World War*. Toronto: Lorimer 1981.

Tepper, Elliott. *Southeast Asia: From Transition to Resettlement*. Ottawa: Canadian Asian Studies Association 1980.

Ujimoto, K. Victor and Gordon Hirabayashi, eds. *Visible Minorities and Multiculturalism*. Toronto: Butterworths 1980.

Walker, James. *The Black Loyalists*. New York: Africana Publishing 1976.

– and Pat Thorvaldson. *Identity: The Black Experience in Canada*. Toronto: Gage 1979.

Winks, Robin. *The Blacks in Canada*. Montreal: McGill-Queen's University Press 1978.

British Immigrants

Akenson, Donald. *The Orangeman: The Life and Times of Ogle Gowan*. Toronto: Lorimer 1986.

Bumsted, J.M. *Land Settlement and Politics on Eighteenth Century Prince Edward Island*. Kingston, Ont.: McGill-Queen's University Press 1987.

Campbell, D. and R.A. MacLean. *1815*. Winnipeg 1982.

– *Beyond the Atlantic Roar: A Study of the Nova Scotia Scots*. Toronto: McClelland & Stewart 1975.

Hibbert, Joyce, ed. *The War Brides*. Toronto: PMA Books 1978.

Jackel, Susan, ed. *A Flannel Shirt & Liberty: British Emigrant Gentle Women in the Canadian West, 1880–1914*. Vancouver: University of British Columbia Press 1982.

Thomas, Peter. *Strangers from a Secret Land: The Voyages of the Brig Albion and the Founding of the First Welsh Settlements in Canada*. Toronto: University of Toronto Press 1986.

Wells, Ronald, ed. *Letters from a Young Emigrant in Manitoba*. Winnipeg: University of Manitoba Press 1981.

European Immigrants

Anderson, Grace. *Networks of Contact: The Portuguese and Toronto*. Waterloo, Ont.: Wilfrid Laurier University Press 1974.

di Giovanni, Caroline Morgan, ed. *Italian Canadian Voices: An Anthology of Poetry and Prose, 1946–1983*. Oakville, Ont.: Mosaic Press 1984.

Ganzevoort, Herman and Mark Boekelman, eds. *Dutch Immigration to North America*. Toronto: Multicultural History Society of Ontario 1983.

Harney, Robert. *Italians in North America*. Toronto: Multicultural History Society of Ontario 1978.

Isajiw, Wsevolod, ed. *Ukrainians in American and Canadian Society*. Jersey City: M.P. Knots Publishing 1976.

Kordan, Bohdan and Lubnmyr Luckiuk, *A Delicate and Difficult Question: Documents in the History of Ukrainians in Canada, 1899–1962*. Kingston: Limestone Press 1986.

Kostash, Myrna. *All of Baba's Children*. Edmonton: Hurtig 1977.

Kovacs, Martin. *Roots and Realities among Eastern and Central Europeans*. Edmonton: Central and East European Studies Association of Canada 1984.

Liddell, Peter, ed. *German Canadian Studies: Critical Approaches*. Vancouver: CAUTG 1983.

Lindstrom-Best, Varpu. *The Finnish Immigrant Community of Toronto, 1887–1913*. Toronto: Multicultural History Society of Ontario 1979.

Marques, Domingues and Joao Medeiros. *Portuguese Immigrants: 25 Years in Canada*. Toronto 1980.

Marunchak, Michael. *The Ukrainian Canadians: A History*. Winnipeg: Ukrainian Academy of Arts and Sciences in Canada 1982.

Pilli, Arja. *The Finnish Language Press in Canada, 1901–1939*. Finland 1982.

Sutherland, Anthony. *The Canadian Slovak League: A History, 1932–82*. Ottawa: Canadian Slovak League 1984.

Yuzyk, Paul. *The Ukrainian Greek Orthodox Church of Canada 1918–51*. Ottawa: University of Ottawa Press 1981.

Zucchi, John E. *Italians in Toronto. Development of a National Identity 1875–1935*. Kingston and Montreal: McGill-Queen's University Press 1988.

Ethnoreligious Immigrants

Kallen, E. *Spanning the Generations: A Study in Jewish Identity*. Toronto: Longman Canada 1977.

Paris, Erna. *Jews: An Account of Their Experiences in Canada*. Toronto: Macmillan 1980.

Peter, Karl. *The Dynamics of Hutterite Society: An Analytical Appraisal*. Edmonton: University of Alberta Press 1987.

Speisman, Stephen. *The Jews of Toronto*. Toronto: McClelland & Stewart 1981.

Immigrant Women

Bohachevsky-Chomiak, Martha. *Feminists Despite Themselves: Women in Ukrainian Community Life, 1884–1939*. Edmonton: Canadian Institute of Ukrainian Studies 1987.

Burnet, Jean, ed. *Looking into my Sister's Eyes: An Exploration in Women's History*. Toronto: Multicultural History Society of Ontario 1986.

Caroli, Betty Boyd et al., eds. *The Italian Immigrant Woman in North America*. Toronto: Multicultural History Society of Ontario 1978.

"Nordic Women." Special issue of *Canadian Women's Studies* (Summer 1988).

CHAPTER FIVE

Native Studies

JOHN A. PRICE

INTRODUCTION

The use of the word "Indian" for the peoples of the western hemisphere is based on the confusion between the Americas and India. The preferred term among the more politically sensitive native people of Canada has become "native." This term reinforces the political point that the native people were here first, and thus have unique aboriginal claims as a charter culture of Canada, alongside the English and French cultures.

Eskimos are also "natives" and "Indians" – just another variation in the broad panorama of subraces, languages, and cultures of the Americas. There is, however, a popular convention in Canada of making a distinction between Eskimos and the other native peoples. There are three Eskimo languages, but the only one in use in Canada is Inuktitut, and in that language the word for "people" is "Inuit," a term which became a standard for the Eskimos of Canada after it was selected for the title of their major political organization, the Inuit Tapirisat of Canada. There is nothing derogatory about using the word "Eskimo," and it is still the conventional term in Alaska.

There were originally many Métis subcultures, since they were the children of whites and the various natives they contacted, particularly in the fur trade. The most common pattern was the marriage of a male French, Scottish, or English trader, or a voyageur, to an Ojibwa or a Cree woman. On the native side, this connection with the trading system helped the Ojibwa and Cree to expand in population and territory to become the two largest and most widely distributed Indian societies in Canada. The Métis who moved into white society tended to become completely assimilated into that society. This was particularly true in Quebec because the French often came to Canada as single males, and participated so completely and for so long in the fur trade. The first formation of a large and distinct Métis society, however, was in the Red River area of Manitoba. Their history is a rather tragic one of discrimination and dispersal, followed in recent years by a revitalization of Métis culture and ethnic associations.

NATIVE HISTORY

Prehistory

Humans entered the New World rather recently – only about 25,000 years ago – coming from Siberia by way of large river valleys in Alaska and Canada that were often ice-free in a time of nearly continent-wide ice sheets. Early finds in the Old World and ethnographic evidence indicate that these early hunters used fire-hardened wooden spears. The addition of stone projectile points to the ends of spears seems to have come into widespread use after about 13,000 BC, after the Yukon-Mackenzie Corridor through the glaciers opened up permanently. Between 6000 and 3000 BC there was an altithermal, a period when the climate was warmer and drier than it is today. Most of the glaciers melted, and over one hundred species of large mammals died out, probably due in part to overkill by the rising population of hunters.

With the rise of human populations and the decline in the number of species of mammals, North American culture underwent a fundamental shift, away from the Paleolithic concentration on hunting large mammals and toward the Mesolithic culture's broadened and intensified use of all available food resources in each environmental niche. Hunting continued, but it expanded to include smaller mammals and birds, and in some environments was even largely replaced by such foods as fish, shellfish, and wild rice. Cultures adapted more to the local environments, and there was much environmentally related inventiveness shown in new forms of housing (igloos, tipis, wigwams, longhouses, and cedar-plank houses), clothing, and transportation (sleds, toboggans, kayaks, birchbark canoes, the round coracle boat in the Plains, and the dugout cedar canoes of British Columbia).

The Archaic is a late Mesolithic culture (about 5000–1000 BC) that is characterized by ground-stone axes to cut wood, a few copper artifacts, and village cemeteries. The northern Shield Archaic extended from the Maritimes across northern Quebec and Ontario to the Keewatin District of the Northwest Territories, and is charac-

terized by caribou hunting. This culture was probably responsible
for the invention of such items as birchbark canoes, snowshoes, and
toboggans, and seems to be the ancestral culture to peoples such as
the Cree, the Montagnais, the Naskapi, and the Micmac. The Laurentian Archaic, in southern Ontario and Quebec, New York, and
Vermont, hunted deer, elk, beaver, and bear. They used the spear
thrower, fished, and used many forest plants. They had cemeteries
in which they placed burial goods with the bodies and covered them
with red ochre. The Ojibwa, with practices such as wild rice gathering, were similar to the Laurentian Archaic peoples when they
were first described by European explorers.

The Arctic Small Tool tradition (3000–1000 BC) is the far-northern
form of the Mesolithic, and comprised whale, walrus, seal, and
caribou hunters above the tree line. A more distinctly Inuit culture
developed in northern Alaska in about 1000 BC, and spread along
the Canadian coasts and into Greenland, Labrador, and Newfoundland, aided by the development of fine skin-covered boats: the small
hunting kayak and the large umiak. This culture had tailored clothing, snow goggles, semi-subterranean houses, oil lamps, and
ground-slate and ivory tools. By the time of the widespread Thule
Inuit of 1000 AD, there were sleds drawn by dogs, harpoons with
sealskin floats, sinew-backed bows, the man's crooked knife and
the woman's semilunar knife, and the tambourine drum.

The subarctic site of Klo-kut, at a caribou-crossing point on the
Porcupine River in the Yukon, shows 1,500 years of Dene-like culture, ancestral to the current Dene-speaking peoples of the region,
such as the Kutchin, the Tutchone, and the Hare. There is continuity
in terms of semi-subterranean houses, serrated and stemmed stone
arrow points, barbed bone arrowheads, fish spears, some copper
projectile points and knives, and birchbark baskets. Broad similar-
ities across the subarctic include snowshoes, toboggans, canoes,
shamanism, bear ceremonialism, fishing weirs, and game drives.

In southern Canada there are three regions in which native societies evolved beyond the level of the simple hunting-band society:
in southern Ontario and Quebec, with the agricultural Iroquoian-
speaking tribes; along the British Columbia coast, with its fishing
tribes and chiefdoms; and the plains, where tribal-level buffalo hunters used horses introduced into the Americas by the Spaniards.

Agriculture was first brought into Canada shortly before 600 AD,
in the Grand River area, probably by the Princess Point people, who
seem to be the ancestors of the Iroquois-speaking Neutrals, Petuns,
and Hurons. They had stone platform pipes, ceramics, small circular
burial mounds, and blade flake tools.

While the agricultural Iroquoian peoples achieved a tribal level of evolution (pan-tribal politics and religion, reciprocal economics, large permanent villages, and so on), several Pacific coast societies went even further and developed to the chiefdom level (centralized politics and religion, redistributive economics, elaborate social rank- ing with slavery, elaborate music and fine arts, and so on). In a worldwide context, these west-coast cultures were the most unusual in Canada in that they were chiefdoms based on fishing rather than agriculture.

Languages

The history of the fifty-four native languages of Canada adds another key dimension to understanding Canadian native history. Beothuk in Newfoundland, Kutenai in southeast British Columbia, and Haida on the Queen Charlotte Islands seem to be "isolates": languages with relationships to other languages that are so ancient, on the order of several thousand years, that we cannot trace the connec- tions. Two are on large islands, and the third is in a mountainous area where enclaves of physical isolation kept these groups culturally separated. Tlingit, of northern BC, is probably a distant member of the Dene or Athapaskan family that occupies the western subarctic of the Yukon, northern BC, and the southern Northwest Territories.

Tsimshian, in northern coastal BC, may be related to the Penutian languages of Oregon, California, and Mexico, hinting at a very an- cient migration. Then there are the Wakashan and Salishan families of languages, which are probably related to each other when we go back far enough in time, to a proposed Mosan phylum of languages. What is now BC was the most linguistically and culturally diversified and historically complex region in Canada in prehistoric times be- cause of its islands, the wealth of its riverain and marine resources, and its ecological diversity.

Inuktitut is relatively recent in Canada, having arrived only about three thousand years ago, and it is related to the Eskimo, Aleut, and Chukitan languages of Alaska and Siberia. The ancient and widespread linguistic family of the eastern subarctic hunters is Al- gonquian, while the Iroquoian languages seem to have spread just in the last 1,400 years into southern Ontario and Quebec with the population expansion that the development of agriculture allowed.

Evolution and Integration

The two most powerful predictors of a native society's behaviour are its aboriginal level of cultural evolution and its current level of integration into Canadian society. These measures of evolution and integration involve a great deal of synthesis of information such as relative population densities and kinds of cultural practices. They are not meant to evaluate cultures in moral or humanistic terms, but they do have a bearing on what kinds of programs will work well in particular kinds of societies. The practical point is that, rather than having an Indian Act that treats all native societies alike, Canada should have legislation that treats them all differently, each according to its particular heritage and needs.

The following table ranks the fifty-four linguistically defined native societies of Canada in rough order by degree of aboriginal cultural evolution or social complexity at the time of extensive white contacts and written descriptions. The terms "band," "tribe," and "chiefdom" are conventional and convenient divisions of the evolutionary continuum that are widely used in social-science theory. The populations given are those of "status Indians" as recognized for federal services by the Department of Indian Affairs and Northern Development (1980). The population data exclude hundreds of thousands of Métis and non-status Indians.

Stages of intersocietal integration are: 1 – first contacts; 2 – low or colonial; 3 – medium or neocolonial; 4 – high or ethnic; and 5 – memory culture. Somewhat different things happen to societies at the various evolutionary levels as they proceed toward integration with a state-level society. For example, under conditions of occupation and domination by a state society anywhere in the world, bands have usually been the most peaceful and acquiescent; tribes have been the most reactive and resistant in the early stages of integration; and chiefdoms have usually been incorporated through the mediation of largely peaceful political and economic processes. Chiefdoms, being close in form to the state, tend to learn quickly how to deal with the state on its own terms. Thus, the chiefdom heritage societies of BC set the pattern for many modern native Canadian political, economic, and artistic developments: first land-claim case against the government (1887); first province-wide political association (1909); first and only labour union (1914); first village tourist facility ('Ksan Dancers); and first restaurant (1972).

Generally, the higher the level of aboriginal evolution of a society, the more quickly it will integrate with a state, but it is not a simple straight-line correlation because of the strong movement to the ethnic level of integration of so many tribal-level societies, several of which came, in the case of Canada, from the United States in the earlier period of militant resistance. Around the world, tribes have often "flip-flopped" from strong resistance to integrated ethnicity. Since the 1970s, the band heritage societies have been leading the

Table 1
Stages* of Aboriginal Evolution and Current
Integration

Societies	Integration	Population
Bands		
Chipewyan-Slave-Yellowknife	2	11,097
Dogrib-Bear Lake-Hare	2	2,461
Loucheux-Kutchin	2	2,600
Nahani-Tanana-Tuchone-Han	2	1,305
Tahltan-Kaska	2	793
Tsetaut	5	Extinct
Naskapi	3	389
Montagnais	3	6,987
Beothuk	5	Extinct
Inuit	2	18,000
Cree	3	92,664
Sekani-Beaver-Sarsi	3	2,197
Micmac	3	11,525
Malecite	3	2,176
Abnaki-Penobscot	3	694
Algonkin	3	4,648
Ottawa	3	1,874
Ojibwa-Saulteaux	3	62,545
Carrier-Chilcotin	3	7,204
Shushwap	3	4,347
Okanagan-Sanpoil-Colville-Lake	3	1,753
Thompson	3	3,023
Lillooet	3	2,961
Tagish	3	?
Nicola	5	Extinct
Kutenai	3	446
Tribes		
Assiniboine	4	1,376
Potawatomi	4	998
Delaware	4	999
Tuscarora	4	841
Gros Ventres	Migrated out of Canada	
Dakota-Sioux	3	6,517
Blackfoot	4	9,875
St. Lawrence Iroquois	5	Extinct
Comox-Seechelt	4	1,534
Songish-Lummi-Clallam-Semiahmoo	4	1,443
Cowichan-Halkomelem	4	7,118
Squamish	4	1,430

Neutral-Erie	5	Extinct
Oneida	4	3,260
Seneca-Cayuga-Onondaga	4	3,680
Mohawk	4	16,640
Huron-Petun	4	1,205
Chiefdoms		
Nitinat	3	442
Nootka	3	3,753
Tlingit	3	552
Niska	3	2,893
Gitskan	3	3,149
Haisla-Kitimat	3	989
Bella Bella-Heiltsuk	3	1,424
Bella Coola	3	730
Kwakiutl	3	3,155
Tsimshian	3	1,560
Haida	3	1,560

*Stages of intersocietal integration: (1) first contacts, (2) low or colonial, (3) medium or neocolonial, (4) high or ethnic, (5) memory culture.

way in pan-Indian movements: 1970 – Inuit Tapirisat founded; 1972 – protests over mercury pollution in Quebec and Ontario; 1973 – the first Arctic Peoples Conference; 1974 – Anicinabe Park occupied; 1975 – Dene Declaration and the James Bay Agreement; 1976 – Mackenzie Valley Pipeline Inquiry; and 1980 – political action by natives led to a promised guarantee of special rights in the new Canadian constitution (still unfulfilled as of 1989).

The following list has an importance beyond evolution, integration, and policy making. It is a reminder of the great cultural diversity of Canada's native peoples, greater in some fundamental ways than those in all the nations of Europe, with major differences in food production, clothing, housing, kinship systems, political systems, arts, religions, and so forth.

A HISTORY OF CANADIAN NATIVE STUDIES

Aboriginal Phase

There have always been intellectuals within native societies – the shamans, elders, and story tellers who commented on their own society and compared it with others. The earliest European explorers, missionaries, and fur traders were directed to these people for information about the various native societies, and later ethnologists cultivated contacts with these "key informants." Many of the most prominent natives in recent history have been contributors to native studies, and even today native people in the academic field of native studies combine the aboriginal tradition with modern scholarship. This intellectual tradition can be demonstrated in the following list of individuals selected from the official Canadian Indian Hall of Fame: Joseph Brant (1742–1807), Mohawk, British Army Officer in the American Revolutionary War, founder of the Six Nations Reserve; Louis Riel (1844–1885), Manitoba Métis, educated in Montreal, elected to the Canadian Parliament but was refused to be seated by Parliament, and led two major resistance movements, for which he was hanged; Peter Martin (1841–1907), Mohawk, trained in medicine at Oxford University, prominent in Iroquoian associations and the Foresters; Pauline Johnson (1862–1913), Mohawk poet; Elmer Jamieson (1891–1972), Cayuga, served in France in World War I, acquired a doctorate in education, and taught at North Toronto Collegiate; James Gladstone (1887–1971), Blackfoot, cattle rancher, president of the Indian Association of Alberta, appointed to the Canadian Senate in 1958; Dan George (1899–1981), Chief of the Squamish Salish, writer, poet, actor in the play *The Ecstasy of Rita Joe* and in eight feature films, notably *Little Big Man.*; George Clutesi (1905–), Nootka, author of such books as *Son of Raven, Son of Deer* (Sidney, BC: Grey's Publishing 1968) and *Potlatch* (Sidney, BC: Grey's Publishing 1969); Andrew T. Delisle (1933–), Mohawk, politician, helped form and run the Indians of Quebec Association; and Frank Calder (1915–), Nishga, politician, first native to be elected to a provincial legislature, in this case to the BC Legislature.

Amateur Phase

Native-studies scholars have an ambivalent attitude toward the amateur beginnings of the discipline, because the material collected is now very valuable, but it was generally badly collected. Archaeology, for example, began in early nineteenth-century antiquarian interests in prehistoric relics. This led to widespread looting and destruction of native cemeteries such as the Dwyer ossuaries north of Hamilton, Ontario, around 1936. Although we are heavily dependent on the early reports of explorers, missionaries, whalers, and fur traders, we know that their information was unorganized, uneven in quality, biased, and poorly understood.

Some of the prominent amateurs were the explorer Samuel de Champlain; a lawyer by the name of Marc Lescarbot; such early

Jesuits as Leclercq, Biard, Rasle, and Brebeuf; and Joseph Lafitau. Reuben G. Thwaites edited *The Jesuit Relations and Allied Documents* (Cleveland: Burrows 1896–1901) into seventy-three volumes. Lafitau is a Jesuit who went beyond observation in an attempt to understand the place of natives in world history. He saw the Hurons and Iroquois as representing an early common state of humankind, and felt that the study of contemporary "primitive" cultures could help us understand ancient cultures, that theories about migration and diffusion had to be based on extensive studies and not the usual speculations, and that "primitive" (primary, early in form) cultures should be judged by their own and not European values. His *Customs of the American Indians* (1724) has been translated from the French and reprinted (Toronto: Champlain Society 1974–1977).

Captain James Cook's records of his visit to Nootka Sound in 1778 contain some valuable information. In 1792, Jose Mozino, the botanist on a Spanish expedition, stayed for four months on Vancouver Island and made an even more important and comprehensive record of Nootka culture. John Gyles became an ethnographer of the Maliseets when he was their captive close to the turn of the eighteenth century. Similarly, John Jewitt was held as a slave of the Nootka and later published a journal of his experiences. An army officer, W.O. Raymond, studied the village of Meductec, where Gyles had earlier been held captive. William F. Ganong analyzed the network of canoe routes and portages of the Northeast.

Paul Kane travelled across Canada from 1849 to 1851 sketching natives, and his journal (1859) and paintings are a valuable record made just prior to extensive changes in the native cultures. Alexander Ross also described the western natives and Métis at around this time. The surveyor David Thompson filled eighty-three notebooks with his observations. Alexander Henry was an early fur trader who recorded many observations on the Cree and Ojibwa. It is records like those of the fur traders (particularly at the Hudson's Bay Company Archives in Winnipeg), and various government accounts (such as those in the National Archives in Ottawa) that provide a wealth of primary data for native studies.

Canadian missionaries taught native languages at a rudimentary level in their primary schools, and learned enough of the language to translate the Scriptures. Father Adrien G. Morice was a Oblate missionary who did some excellent ethnography, history, and linguistics for his day among the Dene, particularly the Carrier in central BC. One missionary, E.F. Wilson in Sault Ste. Marie, corresponded with Franz Boas in 1887, wrote *The Manual of the Ojibwa Language*, and edited *The Canadian Indian* in 1890–91, a journal for

the Canadian Indian Research and Aid Society. Several early ethnologists were active in the Society: Sir William Dawson, its president; George Dawson, who wrote of his work on the Haida; David
Boyle; Alexander Chamberlain; and Horatio Hale.

William Dawson was the principal of McGill University from 1855
to 1893, a geologist, and an amateur archaeologist who excavated
Iroquois remains and related natives to archaeology and the Bible.
His most important excavation was that of Hochelaga, the Iroquoian
village that Champlain visited in the area which later became Montreal.

Daniel Wilson was one of the first professors in Canada to write
on native studies. He was a historian at the University of Toronto
who had an amateur interest in prehistory and wrote *Prehistoric Men*
(1862), which presented New World cultures as fairly shallow in
time but quite separate in development from Old World cultures.
He coined the word "prehistory," and encouraged several Hudson's
Bay Company post managers (such as Bernard Ross at Fort Simpson)
and missionaries (such as Rev. William Kirkby at Fort Yukon) to
make notes and collections of Indian artifacts.

Horatio Hale worked on the us Wilkes Pacific Expedition of 1837–
42, published his data in *Ethnography and Philology* (1842), and then
settled down as a lawyer near the Six Nations Reserve at Brantford,
Ontario, and did ethnology in his spare time. *The Iroquois Book of
Rites* (1883, reprinted New York: AMS 1969) is his most famous publication. Hale also did some work among the Blackfoot and was the
first New World ethnologist to use language as evidence for historical
connections.

Lewis Henry Morgan, a lawyer in Rochester, New York, at this
time, did even more fundamentally important research by putting
Indian ethnology into comparative contexts. His published works
include *League of the Iroquois* (1851, reprinted New York: Corinth
Books 1962); the first scientific study of kinship, *Systems of Consan-
guinity and Affinity of the Human Family* (1870, reprinted Washington:
Anthropological Society 1972); and an influential analysis of cultural
evolution called *Ancient Society* (1877 reprinted Cambridge, Mass.:
Belknap 1964).

Museum Phase

The Geological Survey of Canada was founded in Montreal in 1842,
and its work over the years routinely included notes of archaeological
and ethnographic interest. George M. Dawson became director of
the Geological Survey of Canada in 1895, and contributed to Pacific-

coast ethnology, linguistics, and archaeology. Professional native studies was practised largely out of museums between 1860 and 1940, beginning with the Nova Scotia Museum in Halifax (1868). In 1886, museums were started in Ontario (named the Royal Ontario Museum in 1914) and British Columbia.

Charles Hill-Tout is known for his work around his home near Abbotsford, BC, particularly for the publication of *The Far West, the Home of the Salish and Dene* (London: Constable 1907). His field reports have been collected in *The Salish People: The Local Contribution of Charles Hill-Tout* (Ralph Maud, ed., 4 vols, Vancouver: Talonbooks 1978).

David Boyle was the Ontario Provincial Archaeologist and curator of the Canadian Institute, where he published the *Annual Archaeological Reports of Ontario* from 1886 to 1908. At the suggestion of Franz Boas, he edited *Ethnology of Canada and Newfoundland* (Toronto 1905), the first systematic survey of Canadian ethnology.

Franz Boas worked for most of his career as a professor at Columbia University in the US, but he conducted the major part of his research in Canada, first among the Central Canadian Inuit and then on the BC coast, particularly among the Kwakiutl. He trained dozens of ethnologists, including the Kwakiutl George Hunt, to collect and analyze native ethnography. He maintained a strong influence on Canadian native studies in general, supporting Edward Sapir's appointment to the National Museum of Canada, in 1910, and Marius Barbeau's work on folklore. His Canadian ethnology is readily available today in reprints and collections, such as *The Central Eskimo* (1888, reprinted Lincoln: University of Nebraska Press 1964) and *Kwakiutl Ethnography* (Helen Codere, ed., Chicago: University of Chicago Press 1966).

Alexander Chamberlain, from Peterborough, Ontario, completed a master's thesis in 1889 at the University of Toronto under Daniel Wilson on the Mississauga Indians, a band of Ojibwa who settled into the Toronto region after the land had been emptied by the Iroquois defeat of the Hurons in the mid-1600s. He then went to Clark University in Worchester, Massachusetts, where Franz Boas had taken up his first teaching post. Under Boas's guidance, Chamberlain did some field work among the Kutenai of southern BC; he received the first anthropology doctorate in North America for further work on the Mississauga. He remained on at Clark University when Boas moved to Columbia University.

Edward Sapir was a student of Franz Boas's at Columbia University and came to Canada from 1910 to 1924 as chief of the Anthropology Division of the Geological Survey of Canada. He studied the

Haida, the Nootka, the Tsimshian, and other societies; made major theoretical contributions to understanding how languages change, historical linguistics, and the relationships between language and culture; and supported Leonard Bloomfield's important linguistic research among the Cree. His book *Language* (London: C. Allen & Unwin 1935) is a major classic in linguistics. Sapir encouraged quality publications, intensive studies as well as surveys, studies of the same culture by more than one researcher, the training of native interpreters to record ethnographic material on their own, and the study and recording of native languages, arts, and handicrafts; he opposed close relations with the Department of Indian Affairs in order to avoid spying for that department.

Sapir hired several Columbia University graduates, including Paul Radin, Alexander Goldenweiser, and Frank Speck. They made immense contributions to native ethnology, particularly Speck, who worked boldly, with good rapport with natives and knowledge of their languages, on a great variety of studies in Quebec and Labrador. He provided a flood of articles on such topics as art styles, uses of birchbark, divination, dogs, dreams, game preservation, hunting territories, kinship, mythology, snowshoes, and swimming. One fault with the work produced at this time, and even with that of the next generation of ethnologists, was that they tended to work only toward descriptions of pre-European native cultures and not to describe the native cultures as they actually were at the time of their research. In the first half of the twentieth century, potentially high-quality first-person observations of native cultures were thrown away in favour of reconstructions of a remote and somewhat idealized aboriginal way of life. This left a gap of knowledge when scholars began studying historical acculturation processes after the 1940s.

Marius Barbeau was born in Quebec, studied the classics and law at Laval University, attended Oxford University as a Rhodes scholar in 1907, wrote his thesis on Pacific-coast totemic systems, and did a lot of research out of the National Museum on the Haida, Tsimshian, Huron, Iroquois, and other cultures. His orientation was toward the arts and humanities, and he is considered to be one of the founders of folklore studies in Canada. For example, he established that the floral beadwork designs used by the northeast natives are European in origin. He trained the Tsimshian folklorist William Benyon in how to collect, record, and analyze material.

Francophone anthropology was also later carried on at the National Museum by Carmen Roy and Marcel Rioux. Rioux was involved in creating *Anthropologica*, which was strictly a native-studies journal for several years. He and Roy were interested in collecting folk songs, tales, myths, arts, and crafts, showing a concern with aesthetics and cognitive anthropology rather than with the Boasian tradition of describing cultures in a holistic way. Eventually, this division of interests led to a split at the National Museum into separate ethnology and folklore divisions, each with its own publication series.

Harlan I. Smith was the archaeologist for Boas's Jessup North Pacific Expedition (1897–1899), and became the first archaeologist with the National Museum in Ottawa, for which he took part in excavations right across the country. William J. Wintemberg studied archaeology under David Boyle for about a decade at the Ontario Provincial Museum, made some innovations in site mapping, experimented with techniques of making artifacts, and took on permanent employment in 1911 with Harlan Smith under Edward Sapir in the Anthropology Division of the Geological Survey of Canada at the National Museum in Ottawa, which was called the Victoria Memorial Museum until 1927. His "Distinguishing Characteristics of Algonkian and Iroquoian Culture" (*Bulletin of the National Museum of Canada* 67 (1931): 65–125) became an early standard for North American archaeology.

Diamond Jenness received a diploma in anthropology in 1910 from Oxford University, where he knew Barbeau. He came from New Zealand in 1912 as the anthropologist on the 1913–1918 interdisciplinary Canadian Arctic Expedition led by Vilhjalmur Stefansson. He obtained a position in the National Museum, working at times with native research in all fields of anthropology: ethnology, linguistics, archaeology, physical anthropology, and applied anthropology. He replaced Sapir as curator of the Anthropology Division of the Geological Survey in 1924. He is one of the most important founders of Canadian native studies, and his *Indians of Canada* (Ottawa: F.A. Acland 1932) was a basic reference for decades.

Thomas F. McIlwraith was born in Ontario, received his higher education at Cambridge University, and was the first anthropologist to be appointed full time to a faculty of a Canadian university, in 1925 at the University of Toronto. He worked among the Bella Coola in the 1920s, and is associated with the development of archaeology at the Royal Ontario Museum.

Thus, by the 1930s, even before anthropology was a significant academic subject in universities in Canada, the work of researchers was reaching a consistent professional standard in the hands of people like Knud Rasmussen in the Arctic, Cornelius Osgood in the western subarctic, Frank Speck in the eastern subarctic, Franz Boas on the BC coast, and Diamond Jenness, who moved across the entire country for his research.

Academic Anthropology

After 1940, the primary base of native studies in Canada moved from the museums to the universities. Appointments of professors in native studies have taken place primarily within anthropology, with only a few being made in such fields as history, education, and fine arts. In 1983, about 175, or forty-one per cent, of the 424 full-time anthropology teaching faculty at Canadian universities had some research experience related to North American natives. (Canada had 525 full-time anthropologists in 1983, if those in museums and research institutes are included.) However, only about twenty per cent regularly teach a course on natives somewhere in the Americas, and half of those are in archaeology, the subdiscipline of anthropology that tends to have the weakest integration into multidisciplinary native studies.

The development of a multidisciplinary approach to native studies was delayed until the 1970s, largely because anthropology itself is extremely broad (a generalist discipline), and it inadvertently acquired something of a monopoly on the field. This monopoly was challenged in the 1960s and 1970s by educators and research historians, and then by a broad range of people in the arts and humanities. At the same time, anthropologists were often drawn out of traditional anthropological approaches to native studies, which emphasized descriptions that were reconstructions of the aboriginal way of life, and into acculturation studies, ethnohistory, and applied anthropology.

After 1960, archaeology came to some maturity as a discipline in Canada. Archaeology programs were established in the major universities of each province, and field schools were formally operated. The Canada Council began supporting archaeology in 1961, the Société d'archéologie du Québec was started in 1962, Parks Canada began doing archaeology, and the number of professional archaeologists rose from twelve in 1960, to about two hundred in 1986. William E. Taylor, Jr., became director of the new National Museum of Man (which changed its name to the Canadian Museum of Civilization in 1986) in 1967, and, with James Wright, started the Archaeological Survey of Canada in 1971. By 1986 this survey had published over one hundred archaeological monographs.

While survey work was proceeding in all parts of the country, five large archaeological projects in Ontario served as a training ground for a new generation of archaeologists studying at the University of Toronto: the Jesuit site of Sainte Marie Among the Hurons, directed by Kenneth Kidd in 1941 and Wilfrid Jury in 1948; a large Paleolithic quarry at Sheguiandah, Manitoulin Island, directed by Thomas Lee, in 1951–53; salvage archaeology along the route of the St. Lawrence Seaway, directed by Normal Emerson, in 1956–57; the Serpent Mounds burial site, directed by Richard Johnston, in 1955–60; and the excavation of the Miller Pickering agricultural village, under Walter Kenyon, in 1958–59. A sixth recent project, the Draper site in the area of the proposed Pickering airport near Toronto, is important in terms of the methods used in the complete excavation of a large expanding Huron village.

The Canadian Archaeological Association was started in 1968, first publishing a *Bulletin* and then the *Canadian Journal of Archaeology*, starting in 1977. Legislation covering the protection of antiquities was passed in Ontario in 1952, and in British Columbia in 1960. In 1975, new Canada-wide provincial heritage legislation established licensing requirements for procedures for excavations; set up requirements for comprehensive reporting; emphasized the provincial responsibilities for owning, conserving, studying, and displaying heritage resources; required archaeological studies of lands slated to be developed or disturbed; and limited the role of the Museum of Man's direct work to such federal jurisdictions as the northern territories, national parks, and airports.

Recently, prominent books or monographs in archaeology have been written or edited on British Columbia by Charles E. Borden (*Origins and Development of Early Northwest Coast Culture to about 3,000 B.C.*, Ottawa: National Museums of Canada 1975), Knut R. Fladmark (*British Columbia Prehistory*, Ottawa: National Museums of Canada 1986), and by George F. MacDonald and Richard Inglis (*The Dig: An Archaeological Reconstruction of a West Coast Village*, Ottawa: Archaeological Survey of Canada 1976; they also edited *Skeena River Prehistory*, Ottawa: National Museums of Canada 1979); on the prairies by Anthony P. Buchner (*Cultural Responses to Altithermal (Atlantic) Climate along the Eastern Margins of the North American Grasslands, 5,500 to 3,000 B.C.*, Ottawa: National Museum of Man 1980; he also co-authored *Introducing Manitoba Prehistory*, Winnipeg: Manitoba Department of Cultural Affairs and Historic Resources 1983) and L.F. Pettipas ("A Further Contribution to the Paleo-Indian Prehistory of Manitoba," *Manitoba Archaeological Quarterly* 5, no. 2 (1981): 38–54);

on Ontario by Walter A. Kenyon (*Mounds of Sacred Earth: Burial Mounds of Ontario*, Toronto: Royal Ontario Museum 1986) and Peter L. Storck (*Ontario Prehistory*, Toronto: Royal Ontario Museum 1981); on Quebec by Roger J. Marois (*Les schèmes d'établissement à la fin de la préhistoire et au début de la période historique: le sud du Québec*, Ottawa: National Museum of Man 1974) and James V. Wright (*Quebec Prehistory*, Scarborough, Ont.: Van Nostrand Reinhold 1979); on the Atlantic provinces by James A. Tuck (*Newfoundland and Labrador Prehistory*, Ottawa: National Museums of Canada 1976) and Daniel M. Shimabuku (ed., *1980 Conference on the Future of Archaeology in the Maritime Provinces*, Halifax: Dept of Anthropology, Saint Mary's University 1980); and on the north by Donald W. Clark (*Archaeological Reconnaissance in Northern Interior District of Mackenzie, 1969, 1970 and 1972*, Ottawa: National Museums of Canada 1975) and Robert McGhee (*Canadian Arctic Prehistory*, Toronto: Van Nostrand Reinhold 1978).

Multidisciplinary Phase

The academic model for multidisciplinary programs comes from the American experience in world-area and racial-ethnic studies programs. Although university disciplines were being broken up into specializations, they could be brought back together in both research and teaching by focusing on areas of the world with similar cultures. Advantages are gained in terms of holistic perspectives by bringing together the data and insights on a single cultural tradition from varied disciplines. Racial politics pushed the process along for blacks, Chicanos, and natives in the 1960s, and this movement affected the Canadian scene by the end of that decade.

Trent University created Canada's first Department of Native Studies in 1969. Formal and full interdisciplinary programs are now also located at Laurentian University, Lakehead University, the University of Manitoba, Brandon University, the University of Regina, the University of Saskatchewan, the University of Lethbridge, and several smaller institutions. There are also strong lists of undergraduate native-studies courses at the University of Calgary, the University of Alberta, and Simon Fraser University. American native-studies programs place more emphasis than do Canadian ones on the arts and humanities, and less on language and applied subjects such as politics. Within Canada there is an emphasis on language and fine arts at Brandon University and the University of Lethbridge; on education at Lakehead University and the University of Saskatchewan; and a more general orientation at the schools in central and southern Ontario (Laurentian and Trent universities, respectively). The first native-studies instructors' conference was held in 1983 at the University of Saskatchewan, and estimates at the time of the proportion of native students in native-studies courses ranged widely: University of Saskatchewan – 90%, Brandon University – 75%, University of Manitoba – 50%, University of Lethbridge – 40%, Trent University – 40%, Lakehead University – 20%, Camosun College – 15%, Simon Fraser University – 10%, York University – 10%, and University of Alberta – 7%.

An important dimension of native studies today is ethnohistory. Alfred Bailey studied under Thomas McIlwraith and Harold Innis at the University of Toronto. He carried on the Atlantic tradition of reading the early ethnographies, and wrote *The Conflict of European and Eastern Algonkian Cultures, 1504–1700* (Toronto: University of Toronto Press 1969). Some of the other notable ethnohistorians have been Eleanor Leacock, on the effects of the fur trade on family hunting territories ("Les relations de production parmi les peuples chasseurs et trappeurs des régions subarctiques du Canada," *Recherches amérindiennes au Québec*, 10: 1–2 (1980) 79–90); Harold Hickerson (*Chippewa and their Neighbors: A Study in Ethnohistory*, revised and expanded edition, Prospect Heights: Waveland Press 1988), on the inter-ethnic relations of the Ojibwa (who are also known as the Chippewa); Conrad Heidenreich (*Huronia: A History and Geography of the Huron Indians, 1600–1650*, Toronto: McClelland and Stewart 1971) and Bruce Trigger (*The Children of Aataentsic: A History of the Huron People to 1660*, Kingston and Montreal: McGill-Queen's University Press 1987 [1976]), on the Hurons; Cornelius Jaenen (see the bibliography at the end of this chapter) and Olive Dickason (*The Myth of the Savage and the Beginnings of French Colonialism in the Americas*, Edmonton: University of Alberta Press 1984), on early French-Indian relations; Charles Bishop (*The Northern Ojibwa and the Fur Trade: An Historical and Ecological Study*, Toronto: Holt, Rinehart and Winston of Canada 1974) and Arthur Ray and Donald B. Freeman (*"Give Us Good Measure": An Economic Analysis of Relations Between the Indians and the Hudson's Bay Company before 1763*, Toronto: University of Toronto Press 1978), on natives in the fur trade; D. Bruce Sealey and Antoine Lussier (see bibliography), on the Métis; Robin Fisher (see bibliography), on BC; and Keith Crowe and René Fumoleau (see bibliography), on northern history. Ethnohistory has been going through a major renaissance in the past decade, financed and driven by native land-claims cases across the country, although masses of recently collected data still lie in the filing cabinets of lawyers and native associations.

Quebec

The best colonial context for natives in Canada has been Quebec. In various recent surveys, the Quebec natives had the best housing, the lowest level of social assistance, the lowest rate of off-reserve migration, the highest interracial marriage rate, the highest rate of exclusion of alcoholic beverages from reserves, the lowest suicide rate, the lowest arrest rate, the lowest rate of native militant actions reported in newspapers, a low level of native-association activities and publications, and a general absence of the dysfunctional urban native bar cultures that are so common in British North America.

It may be that the relatively low level of problems recorded among natives in Quebec meant that there was little stimulus there for the development of interdisciplinary native studies. The old Anglo-phone link to science, in contrast to the Francophone link to the humanities and folklore of Sapir and Barbeau, is irrelevant now in Quebec, but it has still been difficult for native studies to develop as an interdisciplinary field within the province's colleges and universities.

Native ethnohistory seems to be well developed in Quebec. Donald B. Smith's analysis *Le Sauvage: The Native People in Quebec Historical Writing on the Heroic Period (1534–1663) of New France* (Ottawa: National Museum of Man, History Division 1974) showed that solid work had been done by men such as Léon Gérin (among the Hurons of Lorette, a suburb of Quebec City), Barbeau, and Jacques Rousseau. Jean-René Proulx and Sylvie Vincent compiled and ana-lyzed data in five volumes in a *Review of Ethnohistorical Research on the Native Peoples of Quebec* (Quebec City: Ministère des Affaires cul-turelles 1985), and Richard Dominique and Jean-Guy Deschênes published a comprehensive bibliographic critique, *Cultures et sociétés autochtones du Québec* (Quebec City: Institut québécois de recherche sur la culture 1985).

Beyond ethnohistory, native studies in Quebec is still largely a subject of anthropology. Thus, there are no departments of native studies at universities in Quebec, as there are in Alberta, Saskatch-ewan, Manitoba, Ontario, and New Brunswick. Only twelve per cent (51 of 429) of the graduate theses done in native studies in Canada from 1972 through 1983 were completed at Quebec's uni-versities, and these were concentrated primarily in traditional an-thropology.

Applied Native Studies

There is a long history of native policies in Canada, but formal and systematic research to arrive at those policies was virtually non-existent. Indian agents would send in reports, and there was some in-house collection of data. There was the occasional speculative article on "the Indian problem" from the time of John McLean's *The Indians of Canada: Their Manners and Customs* (Toronto: William Briggs 1889, facsimile edition: Toronto: Coles 1970). A solid collection of essays did come out of a conference held in 1939, including historian Harold A. Innis's "Expansion of White Settlement in Canada." That work, *The North American Indian Today*, was edited by C.T. Loram and T.F. McIlwraith (Toronto: University of Toronto Press 1943).

Diamond Jenness stands out as an early native advocate within the government who had a genuine understanding of native cultures. He criticized the lack of native consultations in policy formation and the low level of government funding of programs. Since he was born and raised with Maori children in New Zealand, he pressed for the New Zealand model of relations with the Maori to be applied in Canada, with designated seats for natives in the Canadian parliament. At the end of his life he published a five-volume work, *Eskimo Administration* (Montreal: Arctic Institute of North America 1962–1968).

Jenness, Boas, Sapir, and Barbeau all actively protested against the "Potlatch Law," which, from 1882 to 1951, outlawed the practice of potlatch and the "Tasmanawas" dances. Several ethnologists protested against the general repression of native politics and religions, such as the Sun Dances in the prairie provinces (outlawed from 1910 to 1934), peyotism (which briefly came into Manitoba in the 1930s), and the Guardian Spirit ceremonials (among the Salish of northern Washington and southern British Columbia).

In 1964–1966 there was *A Survey of the Contemporary Indians of Canada* (Ottawa: Indian Affairs Branch), directed by Harry B. Hawthorn, of the University of British Columbia, and Marc-Adélard Tremblay, of Laval University, and edited in two volumes by Hawthorn (1966–67). The research on and writing of the Hawthorn-Tremblay Report was done by some fifty Canadian ethnologists, and it became a baseline of data and policy ideas for all subsequent critiques of Canadian native policy. It was a multidisciplinary project, because Hawthorn placed three non-anthropologists from the University of British Columbia in key positions: Stuart Jamieson in economics, Alan Cairns in political science, and Kenneth Lysyk in law. Volume 1 alone, on political and economic policies, made ninety-one recommendations. It called for a long-term special status, "citizens plus," or special-advocacy relationship between the government and native peoples, rather than the simplistic equality and termination-of-federal-services ideas circulating in government at the time.

The federal government attempted to ignore the self-determination orientation of the Hawthorn-Tremblay Report, and came down with a assimilationist Indian Policy "White Paper" in 1969. It was soundly rejected by the native politicians, who used the Hawthorn-Tremblay Report as the basis for their objections, and had to be withdrawn. Slowly, over the past generation, the government has been implementing many policies that were originally recommended in the Hawthorn-Tremblay Report in 1966.

Another major team project was the Program in the Anthropology of Development at McGill University from 1964 to 1976. From 1964 to 1971, Norman Chance directed the project around the theoretical issue of "Does rapid technological change produce anomic value changes?" (See his *Developmental Change among the Cree Indians of Quebec*, Ottawa: Queen's Printer 1970.) The answer is "Not necessarily, if you have the committed involvement of the people whose culture is changing." Then, under Richard Salisbury, the James Bay region of northern Quebec was used as a laboratory for applied anthropology under pressure of the plans to develop hydro-electric dams there. Feedback from research led to a phase of "social animation through research." (See Salisbury's *A Homeland for the Cree: Regional Development in James Bay, 1971–1981*, Kingston and Montreal: McGill-Queen's University Press 1986.) And, finally, the applied anthropologists settled into a pattern of consultant-oriented research. In addition to Chance and Salisbury, some of those who produced books and monographs in Quebec native studies in this period were Bernard Bernier (*The Social Organization of the Waswanipi Cree Indians*, Montreal 1967), Serge Bouchard (comp., *Chroniques de chasse d'un Montagnais de Mingan, Mathieu Mestekosho*, Quebec City: Ministère des Affaires culturelles 1977), Claude Chapdelaine and Norman Clermont (*La maison longue iroquoienne de Lanoraie*, Quebec City: Ministère des Affaires culturelles 1985), Yvon Couture (*Les Algonquins*, Val d'Or, Que.: Éditions Hyperborée 1983), Harvey Feit (*Mistassini Hunters of the Boreal Forest: Ecosystem Dynamics and Multiple Subsistence Patterns*, Montreal 1969), Jo Ann Gagnon (*Le régime de chasse, de pêche et de trappage et les conventions de Québec nordique*, Quebec City: Centre d'études nordiques, Université Laval 1982), Rolf Knight (*Ecological Factors in Changing Economy and Social Organization among the Rupert House Cree*, Ottawa: Queen's Printer 1967), José

Malihot (*Inuvik Community Structure, Summer 1965*, Ottawa: Dept. of Indian Affairs and Northern Development 1968), Toby Morantz (*An Ethnohistoric Study of Eastern James Bay Cree Social Organization, 1700–1850*, Ottawa: National Museums of Canada 1983, and, with Daniel Francis, *Partners in Furs: A History of the Fur Trade in Eastern James Bay, 1600–1870*, Kingston and Montreal: McGill-Queen's University Press 1983), Roger Pothier (*Relations inter-ethniques et acculturation à Mistassini*, Quebec City: Les presses de Université Laval 1967), Richard J. Preston (*Cree Narrative: Expressing the Personal Meanings of Events*, Ottawa: National Museums of Canada 1975), Edward Rogers (*The Material Culture of the Mistassini*, Ottawa: Queen's Printer 1967), Bernard Saladin d'Anglure (with others, *La parole changée en pierre: vie et oeuvre de Davidialuk Alasuaq, artiste inuit du Québec arctique*, Quebec City: Ministère des Affaires culturelles 1978), Rémi Savard (*Le rire précolombien dans le Québec d'aujourd'hui*, Montreal: Éditions Bellarmin 1976), and Adrian Tanner (*Bringing Home Animals: Religious Ideology and Mode of Production of the Mistassini Cree Hunters*, St. John's: Memorial University of Newfoundland 1979).

In the 1970s, dozens of native-studies specialists, such as Michael Asch from Alberta and Hugh Brody from Oxford, became involved in producing reports for and testifying in the Mackenzie Valley Pipeline Inquiry, essentially about how the modernization of the western part of the Northwest Territories should proceed. The inquiry resulted in a very influential report by Justice Thomas Berger, *Northern Frontier, Northern Homeland* (1977). Following the leads of the Hawthorn-Tremblay Report, the McGill Project, and the Berger Inquiry is a new generation of applied-oriented researchers in native studies.

For example, Noel Dyck edited a comparative anthology, *Indigenous Peoples and the Nation State* (St. John's: Memorial University Press 1984). Kathryn Molohon, as editor of *Anthropologica*, has been producing some collections on practical issues, such as education and natives and the media. Barbara Burnaby, a linguist at the Ontario Institute for Studies in Education, published the monographs *Language in Education Among Native Peoples* (Toronto: OISE 1982) and *Promoting Native Writing Systems* (Toronto: OISE 1985). A sociologist, J. Rick Ponting, and a political scientist, Roger Gibbons, did an excellent study of federal native policy and bureaucracy called *Out of Irrelevance: A Sociopolitical Introduction to Indian Affairs in Canada* (Toronto: Butterworths 1980). Sally Weaver did a study of federal native-policy formation using the case of the 1969 White Paper, *Making Indian Policy: The Hidden Agenda, 1968–1970* (Toronto: University of Toronto Press 1981). Adrian Tanner edited *The Politics of*

Indianness: Case Studies of Native Ethnopolitics in Canada (St. John's: Memorial University Press 1983).

Arts, Literature, and Religion

Nancy-Lou Patterson has written a general text, *Canadian Native Art* (Don Mills, Ont.: Collier Macmillan 1973). Some of the books and monographs on the arts are now quite theoretically sophisticated. N. Ross Crumine and Marjorie M. Halpin wrote an influential book, *The Power of Symbols: Masks and Masquerade in the Americas* (Vancouver: University of British Columbia Press 1983). Similarly, Bill Holm's *Northwest Coast Indian Art: Analysis of Form* (Vancouver: Douglas & McIntyre 1978) has been well received. For the north, George Swinton's *Sculpture of the Eskimo* (Toronto: McClelland & Stewart 1982) is excellent.

For recent works on literature, I recommend George F. MacDonald's *In the Shadow of the Raven: The Raven Myth in Polar Cultures* (Vancouver: University of British Columbia Press 1983); Ralph Maud's *A Guide to BC Indian Myth and Legend* (Vancouver: Talonbooks 1982); Robin McGrath's *Canadian Inuit Literature* (Ottawa: Canadian Ethnology Service, No. 194 1984); and Leslie Monkman's *A Native Heritage: Image of the Indian in English-Canadian Literature* (Toronto: University of Toronto Press 1981).

Among recent works on religion, I recommend one monograph on the Cree, two works on the Ojibwa, and two on the Kwakiutl: Adrian Tanner's *Bringing Home Animals;* Selwyn H. Dewdney's *The Sacred Scrolls of the Southern Ojibway* (Toronto: University of Toronto Press 1975); Christopher Vecsy's *Traditional Ojibwa Religion and Its Historical Changes* (Princeton: University of Princeton Press 1983); Irving Goldman's *The Mouth of Heaven: Introduction to Kwakiutl Religious Thought* (New York: John Wiley 1975); and Stanley Walens' *Feasting With Cannibals: An Essay on Kwakiutl Cosmology* (Princeton: University of Princeton Press 1981).

Teaching

While native studies is an important research and applied field in Canada today, it does not fare very well in teaching. Native studies involves only about 0.2% of the faculty positions (66 of 36,000 full-time equivalents) and curricular content in Canadian universities and large colleges. Small colleges typically lack even a single course in native studies. A survey, *Native Studies in Canada*, edited by Robert

S. Allen (Ottawa: Department of Indian Affairs 1982), listed only thirty-three universities and separate colleges in Canada with undergraduate offerings in native studies, housed principally in the following departments: anthropology – 13, history – 9, native studies – 5, and others – 6.

In Canada (as in the US), education was the first discipline outside of anthropology to institute a practical native-studies program, starting at the University of Saskatchewan in 1960, which offered a B.Ed. and then an M.Ed. in Indian and Northern Education. Native education programs then spread to Regina, Brandon, Lakehead, and Western universities, and to the University of Quebec at Chicoutimi. Research on native education is not well developed, having made few advances since the Hawthorn-Tremblay Report of 1966–67. However, prospects are bright, with the appearance of a new two-volume reader and a new native-run, native-education research association called Mokakit.

Of course, every university offers some native-studies courses, but the special programs and departments tend to be in small universities where there are a large number of native students: St. Thomas in New Brunswick; Trent, Laurentian, and Lakehead in Ontario; in Manitoba, Brandon and the University of Manitoba; in Saskatchewan, Regina and the University of Saskatchewan; and Lethbridge in Alberta. The major graduate-level native-studies programs are at York University, in Toronto, which specializes on political and economic issues, and at University of Saskatchewan, which specializes on education and law. Carleton and Trent also have new master's-level native-studies programs.

Publications

Today, about seventy-five books and monographs and about forty graduate theses are produced each year in the field of Canadian native studies. The four western provinces are very strong in this area, producing about one-half of the non-federal publications and fifty-three per cent of the graduate theses. One of the surprising aspects of all this writing is that Canada and the United States virtually ignore each other. About ninety-five per cent of the books, monographs, and graduate theses produced in Canada are confined to Canadian natives, and the same pattern exists for US publications. Similarly, only about five per cent of the reviews in *The American Indian Culture and Research Journal* (University of California, Los Angeles) and *The American Indian Quarterly* (University of California,

Table 2
Publication and Population

	Publication (%)	Population (%)
Eskimoan	26.8	5.4
Algonquian	25.1	45.9
Metis	11.1	23.5
Iroquoian	10.5	6.0
Salishan	7.7	5.7
Athapaskan	7.1	6.5
Wakashan	4.1	2.3
Haida	1.7	0.4
Siouan	1.7	1.9
Tsimshian	1.7	2.2
Beothuk	1.3	0.0
Tlingit	1.1	0.1
Kootenayan	0.2	0.1

Berkeley) are of Canadian books. About twenty-eight per cent of the authors are now women, while only about one per cent of such works were by women thirty years ago.

There is a rough correlation between the amount of publication and audio-visual coverage on the fifty-four native societies of Canada and the size of those societies' populations, except that several extinct societies are still written about and the Inuit are overrepresented. So much work has been done on the Inuit that 125 books and theses were produced in the decade of 1975–1984, about one book or thesis for every two hundred Inuit, and there have been hundreds of articles in such publications as *Inuit Today*, *Études/Inuit/Studies*, and *Arctic Anthropology*. Table 2 illustrates the correlation between the publication of books, monographs, and theses on a group of native societies and their modern populations.

There is very little consistent career development on the part of graduate students in native studies. Thus, outside of archaeology, it is rare for a student to do both a master's thesis and a doctoral dissertation in the field. Only about fifteen per cent of those who do a thesis in native studies remain actively involved in the field.

The following table shows the distribution by specialization of 1,197 books, monographs, and graduate theses produced in Canada in native studies over ten recent years. The major categories are archaeology, history, and cultural anthropology, while there is a pressing need for more work in such fields as economics, religion, sociology, social work, medicine, and psychology. Long-term pros-

Table 3
Native-Studies Specializations (Percentages)

Specialization	Percentage
Archaeology	24
History, Ethnohistory	13
Cultural Anthropology	12
Literature	9
Art, Dance, & Music	8
Politics, Law	8
Education, Texts	6
Linguistics	4
Physical Anthropology	4
Economics, Economy, Anthropology	3
Religion, Philosophy	3
Sociology, Social Work	3
Medicine, Psychology	1

pects also indicate a growing need for college and university teachers in the fine arts and literature sub-fields of native studies. The major producing provinces for theses in native studies have been Ontario (31%), BC (22%), and Alberta (19%), followed by Quebec (12%), and then the other provinces, with only a few percentage points each of the total production.

The Canadian Journal of Native Studies, from Brandon University in Manitoba, is the country's only general native-studies journal, and it is the official journal of the Canadian Indian/Native Studies Association. There are four general anthropology journals: *Anthropologica*, with thirty-three per cent native-studies articles in the last several volumes, from Laurentian University; *Culture*, with thirty per cent native-studies articles, from the Canadian Ethnology Society; *Canadian Journal of Anthropology*, with a predominance of native-studies articles, from the University of Alberta; and *Anthropologie et Sociétiés*, with only six per cent native-studies articles, from Laval University. *Anthropologica* is the only one of the four with a deep backlog of native-studies articles, since it started in 1955 as a native-studies journal.

Canada has six major specialized native-studies journals: *Canadian Journal of Archaeology*, University of Victoria; *Canadian Journal of Native Education*, University of Saskatchewan; *Études/Inuit/Studies*, Laval University; *Native Studies Review*, University of Saskatchewan; *Papers of the Algonquian Conference*, Carleton University; and *Recherches Amérindiennes au Québec*, University of Montreal.

Two monograph series of the National Museum of Man in Ottawa are important sources of technical publications: *Archaeological Survey*, which includes physical anthropology, and *Canadian Ethnology Service* (CES), which includes linguistics studies. There are more than one hundred volumes in each of these series.

The following is a list of one hundred pioneers who have published books in Canadian native studies, arranged initially by specialization and then in a rough chronological sequence. The majority are ethnologists who specialized by culture areas. This list can be used by the reader to track down early publications concerning particular topics or native societies.

Table 4
One Hundred Pioneers in Canadian Native Studies

Author	Subject
General	
Franz Boas	Inuit, Kwakiutl, Tsimshian
Edward Sapir	linguistics, Haida, Nootka, Tsimshian
C. Marius Barbeau	Haida, Huron, Iroquois
Harlan I. Smith	archaeology
William J. Wintemberg	archaeology
Frances Densmore	Ojibwa, Nootka, music
Diamond Jenness	Carrier, Inuit, Ojibwa, Sarcee, Sekani
Thomas F. McIlwraith	archaeology, Bella Coola
Frank G. Speck	Beothuk, Iroquois, Micmac, Montagnais
Paul Radin	mythology
Gertrude Kurath	music, dance
Harold E. Driver	ethnology
Alfred G. Bailey	Algonquian history
Gordon Day	linguistics, history
Richard S. MacNeish	archaeology
William N. Irving	archaeology
Charles E. Borden	Pacific archaeology
Selwyn H. Dewdney	petroglyphs
Marc-Adélard Tremblay	contemporary ethnology, applied
Harry F. Wolcott	education, Kwakiutl
James Wright	archaeology
Cornelius Jaenen	French-native history
Charles Bishop	history, fur trade
Arthur Ray	history, fur trade

Table 4 (suite)
One Hundred Pioneers in Canadian Native Studies

Author	Subject
Rolf Knight	economics, Cree
George Manuel	politics
Harold Cardinal	politics
Pacific	
José M. Mozino	Nootka
Aurel Krause	Tlingit
Charles Hill-Tout	Salish
Edward S. Curtis	Salish, Kwakiutl, Nootka, Haida
John R. Swanton	Haida, Tlingit
Erna Gunther	Klallam
Viola E. Garfield	Tsimshian
Clelland S. Ford	Kwakiutl
George P. Murdock	Haida
Kalvero Oberg	Tlingit
Homer G. Barnett	Salish
Harry B. Hawthorn	British Columbia, applied
Wilson Duff	British Columbia
George Clutesi	Nootka
BC *Plateau*	
Adrien G. Morice	Carrier
James A. Teit	Interior Salish, Klallam
H.H. Turney-High	Kutenai
Irving Goldman	Carrier, Kwakiutl
Prairies	
George B. Grinnell	Blackfoot
Robert H. Lowie	Assiniboine, Chipewyan
Clark Wissler	Blackfoot
Alfred L. Kroeber	Gros Ventres
Oscar Lewis	Blackfoot
John C. Ewers	Blackfoot
David Mandlebaum	Plains Cree
Lucien Hanks and Jane Hanks	Blackfoot
Hugh A. Dempsey	Blackfoot
John Snow	Assiniboine history
Iroquoia	
Gabriel Sagard	Huron
Joseph Lafitau	Iroquois, Huron
Louis H. Morgan	Iroquois
Horatio Hale	Iroquois
Arthur C. Parker	Iroquois
William N. Fenton	Iroquois
Elizabeth Tooker	Huron
Anthony F. Wallace	Seneca, religion

Table 4 (suite)
One Hundred Pioneers in Canadian Native Studies

Author	Subject
Bruce G. Trigger	Huron, archaeology, history
Conrad Heidenreich	Huron, history, geography
Western subarctic	
Emile F. Petitot	Chipewyan, Hare, Inuit, Kutchin
Pliny E. Goddard	Beaver, Chipewyan, British Columbia
Cornelius G. Osgood	Han. Ingalik, Kutchin, Tanaina
John Honigmann and Irma Honigmann	Inuit, Kaska, Slave
June Helm	Dogrib
Richard Slobodin	Kutchin, northern Métis
Eastern subarctic	
John Gyles	Maliseet
Alanson B. Skinner	Ojibwa, Cree
John M. Cooper	Northern Algonquians
Leonard Bloomfield	Cree linguistics
Regina Flannery	Eastern Cree
Inez Hilger	Ojibwa
Jacques Rousseau	Cree
Irving A. Hallowell	Abenaki, Ojibwa, Saulteaux
Ruth Landes	Ojibwa, Potawotomi
Eleanor Leacock	Montagnais
Harold Hickerson	Ojibwa
Wilson Wallis and Ruth Wallis	Micmac, Malecite
Edward S. Rogers	Ojibwa, Cree
Philip Bock	Micmac
Richard Salisbury	Cree, applied
Richard J. Preston	Cree
Adrian Tanner	Cree
Basil Johnston	Ojibwa history and folklore
Arctic	
Knud Rasmussen	Inuit
Kaj Birkett-Smith	Inuit
Frank G. Vallee	Inuit
Asen Balikci	Inuit
Jean L. Briggs	Inuit
David Damas	Inuit
Milton Freeman	Inuit, applied
Nugligak	Inuit
Peter Pitsesolak	Inuit history

SELECTED BIBLIOGRAPHY OF
BOOKS PUBLISHED SINCE 1970

Bibliographies

Corley, Nora T. *Resources for Native Peoples Studies*. Ottawa: National Library
of Canada 1984.
A description of the major library holdings and archives on Canada's
native peoples, including periodicals and audio-visuals. Includes a topical
bibliography.
Murdock, George P. and T.J. O'Leary. *Ethnographic Bibliography of North
America*. 4th ed. 5 vols. New Haven: HRAF Press 1975.
This is the basic bibliography on traditional ethnographic research, organized by names of the native societies.

General

Cox, Bruce, ed. *Cultural Ecology: Adaptations of Canadian Indians, Inuit, and
Metis*. Ottawa: Carleton University Press 1986.
A general reader on ecology, ethnology, history, and politics. Includes a
topical bibliography.
Morrison, R. Bruce and C. Roderick Wilson, eds. *Native Peoples: The Canadian
Experience*. Toronto: McClelland & Stewart 1986.
This is an anthropological reader with brief surveys of archaeology and
linguistics, and coverage of ethnology by culture areas. Most of the chap-
ters are concerned with historical cultural changes.
Price, John A. *Native Studies: American and Canadian Indians*. Scarborough,
Ont.: McGraw-Hill Ryerson 1978.
An interdisciplinary review that spans archaeology, linguistics, ethnol-
ogy, history, sociology, and practical issues in politics, economics, and
education. Includes chapters on such topics as religion, the arts, urban-
ization, and stereotyping in motion pictures.
Sturtevant, William C., general editor. *Handbook of North American Indians*.
Washington, DC: Smithsonian Institution 1978. (*Arctic* volume edited by
David Damas, *Subarctic* by June Helm, and *Northeast* by Bruce Trigger.)
These large volumes consist of detailed and technical articles that sum-
marize the traditional anthropological research in each region. Future
volumes will cover the northwest coast, the plateau, and the plains.

Education

Barman, Jean, Yvonne Hebert, and Don McCaskill, eds. *Indian Education in
Canada*. 2 vols. Vancouver: University of British Columbia Press 1986.

This collection was edited by a historian, a linguist, and a sociologist. The first volume, *The Legacy*, has articles on the history of native education and takes case studies from across the country. The second volume, *The Challenge,* deals with contemporary issues.

Ethnology

Balikci, Asen. *The Netsilik Eskimo*. Garden City, NY: Natural History Press 1970.
A well-written analysis of traditional Inuit life.

Mandlebaum, David G. *The Plains Cree*. Regina: Canadian Research Centre 1979.
Some of the Cree left the northeast forests and entered the plains in historic times, so they make an interesting historical study.

Stearns, Mary Lee. *Haida Culture in Custody: The Masset Band*. Vancouver: Douglas & McIntyre 1981.
The modern kind of ethnology that tries to understand aboriginal historical *and* contemporary life.

History

Crowe, Keith J. *A History of the Original Peoples of Northern Canada*. Montreal: McGill-Queen's University Press 1974.
A unique synthesis of northern history.

Fisher, Robin. *Contact and Conflict: Indian-European European Relations in British Columbia, 1774–1890*. Vancouver: University of British Columbia Press 1977.
Fisher has written four chapters in a general historical sequence and four thematic chapters: "Image of the Indian," "Gold Miners and Settlers," "Missionaries," and "Government Administrators."

Fumoleau, René. *As Long As This Land Shall Last: A History of Treaty 8 and 11, 1870–1939*. Toronto: McClelland & Stewart 1975.
A careful historical documentation of treaty making in the north by a priest who has been a long-standing advocate of northern native peoples.

Jaenen, Cornelius J. *Friend and Foe: Aspects of French-American Cultural Contact in the Sixteenth and Seventeenth Centuries*. Toronto: McClelland & Stewart 1976.
The best general survey of early French-Indian relationships in Canada.

Rowe, Frederick W. *Extinction: The Beothuks of Newfoundland*. Toronto: University of Toronto Press 1977.
The best of several works on the history of the extinction of the Beothuks.

Sealey, D. Bruce and Antoine S. Lussier. *The Métis: Canada's Forgotten People*. Winnipeg: Manitoba Métis Federation Press 1975.

Métis scholarship has boomed, along with the great expansion in Métis ethnic organizations and land claims, but this early work still stands up well as a basic review of the Métis of Manitoba and Saskatchewan.

Trigger, Bruce G. *Natives and Newcomers: Canada's Heroic Age Reconsidered.* Montreal & Kingston: McGill-Queen's University Press 1985.

Trigger is an archaeologist who has become the pre-eminent ethnohistorian on early eastern Canada. This is a broad synthesis of archaeology, ethnology, and history. Woven throughout the text are discussions of the changing perspectives in native studies. Thus, for example, the first chapter is a history of Canadian historical writings.

Politics, Social Work, and Law

Breton, Raymond and Gail Grant, eds. *The Dynamics of Government Programs for Urban Indians in the Prairie Provinces.* Montreal: Institute for Research on Public Policy 1984.

Urban native programs in Alberta, Saskatchewan, and Manitoba; a summary of Canada's native policy; and a comparison of US and Canadian native policies and programs.

Morse, Bradford W., ed. *Aboriginal Peoples and the Law: Indian, Métis and Inuit Rights in Canada.* Ottawa: Carleton University Press 1985.

A collection by Canada's leading native-law specialists dealing with aboriginal rights, treaties, the Constitution, provincial laws, reserve lands, taxation, land claims, and the James Bay and other comprehensive agreements.

Ponting, J. Rick, ed. *Arduous Journey: Canadian Indians and Decolonization.* Toronto: McClelland & Stewart 1986.

A collection dealing with economic development, aboriginal rights and claims, and self-government, particularly from sociological, political-science, and government-policy perspectives.

CHAPTER SIX

Amerindian Studies in Quebec

RICHARD DOMINIQUE

Although there are already surveys, assessments, and debates on native studies in Quebec that permit scholars to further their research,[1] no analysis of the main orientations has been produced within a context allowing for a better grasp of the specific nature of Quebec's contribution to native studies. This retrospective attempts to situate the achievements, deficiencies, and major trends presently found in Quebec Amerindian studies. It describes native studies in Quebec on a general level, rather than providing a list of individuals and bibliographical references. In brief, at a moment when Quebec Amerindian studies is undergoing a questioning of its development and orientations, this article seeks to highlight some elements for a constructive critique of the field.

Within this discussion, the expression "native studies in Quebec" refers to Quebec Francophones and Anglophones who have undertaken and produced research on the native peoples of North America. Three major periods of study can be identified: the forerunners, the professionalization of researchers, and the diversification of centres of research. For a better definition of Quebec scientific research in the native environment, the only studies taken into consideration have been those that are analytical and produced by scholarly research. Work in the fields of medicine, biology, and epidemiology have been excluded, while publications on physical anthropology, psychology, archaeology, and linguistics have been touched on briefly within existing studies. The principal body of information for this retrospective is taken from the results of research touching on themes that are dealt with in ethnology and in the human and social sciences.

THE FORERUNNERS (1850–1959)

Until 1960, few Quebec researchers took an interest in native cultures to the extent that they became one of the main leitmotifs of their careers. Two exceptions were Marius Barbeau and Jacques Rousseau. Barbeau, working at the National Museum of Canada, published over sixty studies on the oral tradition, languages, institutions, arts, and mythology of the Tshimshians, Eastern Kutchin, Hurons, and Iroquois. His works were essentially descriptive and centred on preserving native authenticity. Rousseau was the first Francophone scientist to study the ethnology of the Algonquians of the subarctic. He wrote over fifty articles, some in collaboration with his wife Madeleine, on their alimentation, material culture, social organization, and religion.

During this period, other researchers also contributed to a knowledge of native cultures through the occasional article or book on Amerindian groups living near urban centres. Their major themes were history, the description of distinctive cultural traits, and the geographical distribution of native peoples. The most significant contributions of the time, however, were those made by American researchers, which today constitute the fundamental references for a knowledge of native cultures.

THE PROFESSIONALIZATION OF RESEARCHERS (1960–1974)

From 1960, a clear break appears in native studies in Quebec. Prior to 1960, the National Museum of Canada was the only organization that hired Quebec researchers to carry out scientific studies on native societies. But with the expulsion of Jacques Rousseau from the Museum by an order-in-council, the expansion of Quebec universities, the development of the public administration, and the industrial exploitation of the north, an entirely new context was created.

Since the end of World War II, the Canadian government has given serious consideration to the socio-economic conditions of native peoples and to developing the Canadian north. For Quebec, these issues became all the more explosive during the Quiet Revolution of the 1960s. The north became a choice terrain for Quebec researchers, and the paths opened by Marius Barbeau and other forerunners, with the exception of Rousseau, were momentarily abandoned. Only the archaeologists continued to take a certain interest in native groups near urban centres, as they began to study the former occupants of the Saint Lawrence Valley.

The universities and the public administration became career centres for research professionals. During the 1960s, research centres were established, projects were set up, young researchers were trained. The relationship between government and the academic environment was such that university professors participated actively in government committees studying the modern living conditions of Canadian natives and the legal-social dimension of natives. Several university students and researchers were hired to work on these committees.

Within this context, research moved away from vast monographs to concentrate on developing specific themes. Government intervention in the north led to speculation regarding the consequences of contact between native cultures and North American industrialized society.

The first major project, undertaken at McGill University, was the McGill Cree Project, which laid the foundations for the present-day "Programme in the Anthropology of Development." The principal objectives were to analyze the historical origins of underdevelopment and the modification of the James Bay Crees' forms of adaptation, so as to propose strategies of development and change that would take into account the rights of native peoples to a separate and distinct culture. In the same vein, the Northern Coordination and Research Centre of the Department of Northern Affairs and National Resources established a research project on the development of the MacKenzie Valley, for which it hired a number of Quebec researchers.

On a more academic level, the influence of French structuralism and American cognitive anthropology moved some Quebec researchers to set up groups for the study of native symbolism. The Laboratoire d'anthropologie amérindienne explored the connections between oral tradition, taxonomy, and ritual among the Montagnais. Simultaneously, the founders of the Association Inuksiutiit Katimajiit, Inc., developed diverse projects aimed at a systematic analysis of the traditional life and territorial occupation of the Inuit of Nouveau-Québec. The Association produced studies of communities, analyses of Inuit knowledge, and thematic studies on toponymy, genealogy, and ethnohistory that covered the entire territory. Based at Laval University, this group today publishes *Études/Inuit/Studies* and *Inuksiutiit allaniagait*, and organizes a biennial international conference on contemporary eskimology.

In 1971, the creation of the journal *Recherches amérindiennes au Québec* provided a forum for the exchange and pooling of research among Quebec researchers working in native issues. Henceforth, native studies in Quebec were no longer the result of individual efforts but of a collaboration among research professionals.

THE DIVERSIFICATION OF RESEARCH CENTRES (1975–PRESENT)

The announcement of industrial mega-projects throughout the 1970s was a controversial issue that reoriented native studies. The James Bay Hydro Project in northern Quebec caused impact evaluations to be commissioned on a number of fronts. Other large-scale projects of the same nature had already taken place in the regions of Haute-Mauricie, Lac Saint-Jean, and Côte-Nord without causing such heated debate among Amerindians as that surrounding the James Bay Project; indeed, James Bay permitted a crystallization of trends already in process, leading to the bureaucratization and politicization of the native environment.

During the 1970s, native organizations and government administrations developed their political argument with the help of experts from several disciplines. New research centres came into being; native agencies, multipartite committees, and advisory firms all trained a number of professional researchers. On the native side, the majority of research tends to support unequivocally the occupation of the entire territory and the importance of systems of land use. The native peoples wish to prove the persistence of their culture and their wish to develop it. As part of the negotiation process, studies are commissioned to prove the contribution of renewable resources to the economy of native communities. With the implementation of agreements, the concerned parties want to keep a close eye on events so as to evaluate their interventions and the balance of power. Program-evaluation studies are produced, along with studies establishing technical parameters for the exploitation of territory. In a larger sense, this context allows researchers to analyze the articulations possible between hunting societies and industrial states. However, access to reports issued both by native groups and by government and semi-public groups is difficult, as these parties control the circulation and publication of their findings. Such a lack of public information does nothing to improve the quality of debate, and encourages the propagation of clichés and prejudices.

The James Bay Project raised debate in the world of Quebec Amerindian experts on the following issue: What can a specialist in Amerindian studies offer in the way of expertise that is neither traditional, stereotypical studies, nor empirical studies carried out for date compilation? In other words, is it possible to carry on a scientific discourse on the social implications of northern development?

Most of the more recent studies have been commissioned by government administrations for the purpose of identifying their clientele and establishing programs. Today, several departments at various levels of government, paragovernmental agencies, and all kinds of associations, including native ones, intervene in the issue and claim resources and powers. Each, in its own manner, demands part of the responsibility and imputability, and invests in research studies to prove the worthiness of its actions. Moreover, those requesting these studies want an immediate solution to isolated problems. Studies of impact and of political claims can be taken as an example. Such studies are already structured from the time they are commissioned, as the terms of reference have already been laid down by the promoters and administrators concerned.

The native environment is probably the only field of research in which political and governmental authorization is required in order to obtain funding for research. This political consideration can in fact influence the research itself, and it implies a certain lack of funding agencies. One of the consequences is a marked decrease in fieldwork studies in fundamental research. It is still possible to carry out fieldwork studies today, providing that the study is well enough defined so that the concerned population can grasp its purpose. However, the need for political recommendations leads one to doubt the critical capacity of evaluators. The limits and constraints imposed by fieldwork research are part of the risk and beauty of the profession – but when funds are refused for want of political support, the path is open to mediocrity. Institutions that administer research funding would do well to examine this problem and to develop criteria that take into account scientific values rather than political and administrative considerations.

The current methods of control cast doubt upon the credibility of research on Amerindian and Inuit issues. In theory, the same data submitted to the same analytical processes should furnish similar results. This scientific prerequisite is virtually absent from Quebec Amerindian studies. Access to data remains difficult, as they are too often considered political by administrators. Under these circumstances, the publication of results becomes increasingly complex and makes difficult an adequate scientific evaluation. Consequently, researchers and the public in general are deprived of an essential element for the advancement of knowledge and the refining of the debate.

One of the tasks of scientific research is to go beyond daily observation and instantaneous explanation. With the help of methodological observations, it establishes links between apparently unrelated realities; it attempts to reveal the hidden reality. From this stance, the goal of researchers has little in common with those of administrators and politicians, for the scientist must break down, rather than build up, the ideologies that shape the apparent reality. Such a procedure can contradict official statements and give rise to much discussion. Presently, little dissonance is heard in the native environment, and this is perhaps a revealing statement on the integrity of the research.

Universities have traditionally been centres in which a certain intellectual freedom permitted the development of fundamental research. The establishment of research centres allowed professionals to work according to the procedures of scientific methods. Yet, in Quebec, not one university research centre has permanently incorporated professionals in Amerindian and Inuit research. Often, those projects governed by professors include students who can thus complete their theses. These projects last only the duration of a grant or bursary, and no university centre has been able to establish professional expertise based on the contribution of senior researchers. Over the last fifteen years, research has increasingly taken place in organizational environments, with universities and museums taking a back seat in terms of production. Consequently, universities today have a hard time participating in current debates on Amerindian and Inuit studies.

The study of classical themes and ethnohistorical research continues in the academic environment, a context in which staff and budgets are channelled into the application of government conventions and programs. However, specialized programs in native studies are becoming increasingly visible on the college and university scene. Based on the Anglo-Saxon approach to "Native Studies," this trend groups within one institution all aspects of the native environment, and offers the package to its clientele within a certificate program. Does this concentration encourage a better understanding of native cultures and societies, or does it isolate them from the social and historical phenomena that affect the body of humanity? In other terms, does native studies collaborate, as do other fields of study, in the development of approaches and models that attempt to explain the social and human reality? Fundamentally, could it observe social and cultural phenomena without necessarily being a privileged, outlying area of knowledge?

Quebec Amerindian studies is at an important crossroads. On the one hand, studies are diversifying considerably, which should create a source of fertile, efficient findings. On the other hand, researchers do not have the instruments allowing for a mutual influence as they make their findings a common ground for hypotheses and answers. This absence of a common pooling of data, development of theories, elimination of guesswork, and evaluation of production is making itself more and more felt in the field of native studies.

CONCLUSION

Until 1960, Quebec Amerindian studies were coloured by a historical-cultural approach aimed principally at describing the distinctive cultural traits and geographical distribution of native groups. Then social change, acculturation, and traditionalism became the major themes. The use and testing of theoretical models was emphasized. Quebec research professionals organized and concentrated their studies on the subarctic and arctic populations, with the exception of a group of archaeologists who studied the Iroquois of the Saint Lawrence Valley. Universities and government were the homes of the majority of Quebec Amerindian specialists during these years.

With the signing of the James Bay and Northern Quebec Agreement, a third period began, which had already been apparent as of the mid-1960s. Native studies were increasingly carried out within various organizational structures, while universities seem to specialize in ethnohistory and to offer specialized study certificates.

In its theory and methodology, Quebec Amerindian studies does not seem to differ from Amerindian studies in the rest of North America, except for a structuralist contact which has led certain authors to define a division between Francophone and Anglophone researchers. A fundamental distinction, however, characterizes Quebec Amerindianism: contrary to the United States and the rest of Canada, where native-studies research began in the museums and spread to the universities and later to the political and administrative environment, native studies in Quebec had its source in the interrelation between public administration and the universities.

Currently, the majority of Quebec Amerindianists work outside of the academic environment, and are found in or around public administration. While this situation is original and creative, it can lead to the isolation of research and cast doubt upon the scientific integrity of researchers, unless there is a common ground where researchers can exchange ideas and carry out fundamental research.

An improvement in both the scientific and political discourses on the sociological realities of native peoples must lie in a discussion of what native societies can be, and what they must become. Professional researchers in the Amerindian and Inuit environments must follow, enrich, and make public the "minutes" of these discussions in order to encourage a new perception of native peoples.

NOTES

1 See, for example, Asen Balikci, "Commentaires: Faux combats, tristes arènes," *Recherches amérindiennes au Québec* 10, no. 1–2 (1980): 123; Asen Balikci, "Commentaires: La recherche en sciences sociales en milieu autochtone," *Recherches amérindiennes au Québec* 15, no. 4 (1985): 93–4; Serge Bouchard, "Faux combats, tristes arènes: réflexion critique sur l'amérindianisme d'aujourd'hui," *Recherches amérindiennes au Québec* 9, no. 2 (1979): 183–94; Richard Dominique, "La recherche en sciences sociales en milieu autochtone," *Recherches amérindiennes au Québec*, 15, no. 4 (1985): 92–3, 99–100; Richard Dominique and Jean-Guy Deschênes, *Cultures et sociétés autochtones du Québec: bibliographie critique* (Quebec City: Institut québécois de la recherche sur la culture 1985); Louis-Jacques Dorais, "La recherche sur les Inuit du Nord québécois: bilan et perspectives," *Études/Inuit/Studies* 8, no. 2 (1984): 99–115; Jean-François Moreau, "Dix ans de recherches amérindiennes au Québec," *Recherches amérindiennes au Québec* 11, no. 2 (1981): 155–60; Jean-Jacques Simard, "Commentaires: La recherche en sciences sociales en milieu autochtone," *Recherches amérindiennes au Québec* 15, no. 4 (1985): 97–9; Marc-Adélard Tremblay, "La recherche universitaire nordique dans les sciences humaines au creux de la vague," *Recherches amérindiennes au Québec* 14, no. 3 (1984): 90–5; and Marc-Adélard Tremblay, "Les études amérindiennes au Québec, 1960–1981: État des travaux et principales tendances," *Culture* 2, no. 1 (1982): 83–106.

The following is a list of twenty books that attest to Quebec's contribution to native studies. This is a subjective selection, and it does not take into account the articles, theses, and reports that have been published in the field. However, a consultation of the journals *Recherches amérindiennes au Québec*, *Études/Inuit/Studies*, *Anthropologie et sociétés*, *Paléo-Québec et Antropologica* would constitute a good introduction to the subject.

Balikci, Asen. *The Netsilik Eskimo*. Garden City: Natural History Press 1970.
Barbeau, Marius. *Huron and Wyandot Mythology*. Ottawa: Department of Mines 1915. (Memoirs of the Canadian Geological Survey, 80.)

– *Totem Poles*. Ottawa: National Museum of Canada 1950–51. (Bulletin no. 119. Anthropological Series No. 30, 2 vols.)

Bouchard, Serge, comp. *Chroniques de chasse d'un Montagnais de Mingan, Mathieu Mestekosho*. Quebec City: Ministère des Affaires culturelles 1977.

Chance, Norman, ed. *Developmental Change Among the Cree Indians of Quebec, McGill Cree Project (ARDA Project no. 34002)*. Ottawa: Rural Development Branch, Department of Forestry and Rural Development 1968.

Clermont, Norman, Claude Chapdelaine and Georges Barré. *Le site iroquoien de Lanoraie: témoignage d'une maison-longue*. Montreal: Recherches amérindiennes au Québec 1983.

Delâge, Denys. *Le pays renversé. Amérindiens et Européens en Amérique du nord-est 1600–1664*. Montreal: Boréal Express 1985.

Desrosiers, Léo-Paul. *Iroquoisie*. Montreal: Étude de l'Institut d'histoire d'Amérique française 1947.

Duhaime, Gérard. *De l'igloo au H.L.M., Les Inuit sédentaires et l'État Providence*. Quebec City: Centre d'études nordiques, Université Laval 1985.

Francis, Daniel and Toby Morantz. *Partners in Furs. A History of Fur Trade in Eastern James Bay 1600–1870*. Montreal and Kingston: McGill-Queen's University Press 1983.

Guy, Camil. *Le canot d'écorce de Weymontaching*. Ottawa: Musées nationaux du Canada, Musée national de l'Homme 1970.

LaRusic, Ignatius E. et al. *La négociation d'un mode de vie. La structure administrative découlant de la Convention de la Baie James: l'expérience initiale des Cris*. Montreal: ssDcc Inc. 1979.

Malaurie, Jean et Jacques Rousseau, eds. *Le Nouveau-Québec. Contribution à l'étude de l'occupation humaine*. Paris, La Haye: Mouton 1964.

Maurault, Joseph P.A. *Histoire des Abénakis depuis 1605 jusqu'à nos jours*. Sorel: L'Atelier typographique de la Gazette de Sorel 1866.

Saladin d'Anglure, Bernard. *La parole changée en pierre. Vie et oeuvre de Davidialuk Alasuaq, artiste inuit du Québec arctique*. Quebec City: Ministère des Affaires culturelles 1978.

Savard, Rémi. *Le rire précolombien dans le Québec d'aujourd'hui*. Montreal: L'Hexagone/Parti Pris 1977.

Sévigny, P. André. *Les Abénaquis: Habitat et migrations (17e et 18e siècles)*. Montreal: Éditions Bellarmin 1976.

Tanner, Adrian. *Bringing Home Animals. Religious Ideology and Mode of Production of the Mistassini Cree Hunters*. London, Ont.: Hurst and Co. Ltd./ Institute of Social and Economic Research, Memorial University of Newfoundland 1979.

Trigger, Bruce G. *The Children of Aataensic: A History of the Huron People to 1660*. Montreal: McGill-Queen's University Press 1976.

Vincent, Sylvie et Bernard Arcand. *L'image de l'Amérindien dans les manuels scolaires du Québec*. Montréal: HMH 1979.